THE GLORIOUS RESPONSIBILITY OF HAPPINESS

*The Little Book of Daily Inspirations to Embrace Your
Spine-Tingling Adventure Towards a Happy Life*

ALI WILLIAMS

The Glorious Responsibility of Happiness
Copyright © 2022 by Ali Williams

All rights reserved. No part of this publication may be reproduced, distributed, or transmitted in any form or by any means, including photocopying, recording, or other electronic or mechanical methods, without the prior written permission of the author, except in the case of brief quotations embodied in critical reviews and certain other non-commercial uses permitted by copyright law.

Tellwell Talent
www.tellwell.ca

ISBN
978-0-2288-8712-6 (Paperback)

DEDICATION

This book is dedicated to all the women who give everything to everyone else and deny themselves permission to come first.

For all the mums, stepmums, sisters, wives, partners, daughters, aunts, and nieces who are powerful beyond their knowing.

For my Mum, who suffered so much throughout her short life. For the day I stood at the end of her bed as a 16-year-old, watching her laboured breathing, as she beckoned me to sit next to her, and shared her wisdom in a moment that would last a lifetime. "Take every opportunity you get," she said.

For all the motherless daughters, childless mothers, women who have decided not to have children, daughters of disfunction, women experiencing adversity, and anyone who has been through trauma.

To all the grandmothers who came before us, surviving through times that shamed women for speaking out. The ones who suffered in silence and wished they could stand up for themselves but were afraid to. To the pioneers who called out the patriarchy and put their lives, reputations, and relationships on the line to inspire change. Thank you to all of them for giving birth to our mothers, who then gave birth to us, the guardians of the future. And for my two grandmothers, one of whom wished she used her voice, and the other who carried the lifelong heaviness of a family secret.

For my beautiful daughter and stepdaughters and their generation, may this book serve as a reminder you are always enough. These powerful young women fuel my unwavering determination to encourage them to embody their desires and empowerment. May their strength, dreams and passions lead the way for not only their own fulfilment, but for those who follow, so the future is one of joyful possibility rather than the blah of probability.

INTRODUCTION

Through my own lived experience of trauma, self-loathing, and many years of feeling the world would be better off without me, I finally found my way to self-love, acceptance, and the smile-at-myself-in-the-mirror level of happiness. But I chose the long way.

My mother and grandmother both passed away from breast cancer when I was 16. I put on a brave face but was more affected than I was capable of admitting which resulted in many years of unreconciled grief and self-destruction.

My long list of coping mechanisms included alcohol, cigarettes, and marijuana. I partied my way into oblivion every weekend and existed on a diet of resentment, anger, and disastrous relationships.

At one point I ended up in hospital with a complete body shutdown and serious illness.

"Oh great, here I go again today. My life is crap," was my default internal dialogue. I ruminated over these destructive thoughts as I lived through the daily grind. I internalised a damaging aversion to any kind of hope with that sinking feeling in my belly each day I opened my eyes. There was heaviness in my heart that pulled me back down through the mattress and the only way out of bed was to slide out sideways until the floor met my body. On those days it was difficult to breathe, and I landed heavy on the ground with every footstep.

I was reactive to other people's behaviour which created difficult relationships with friends and work colleagues. I was resistant to rules and requirements and spoke out when I thought I, or anyone, was being excluded or unfairly treated, regardless of whether it was rational or true. I was living the contrast of both rage and vulnerability, questioning why no one understood me. I believed I was unlovable and that was my destiny.

After a serious brain fart period of poor judgement at age 26, I married a man who I knew was never going to be supportive but did it anyway. Nine years later (and three beautiful kids – totally worth it), after tiring of being told I was, "Fucked in the head," I left. It was the first time in my life I stepped up to own my self-worth. The moment I said, "It's over," my body was flooded with relief. The saying, "I felt the weight lift off my shoulders," is real.

I took ownership of my story during this time and began working on myself. I was healing, and gave myself permission to prioritise my wellbeing.

I took responsibility for my life and my happiness.

Several years later I married an amazing man, and we became the Brady Bunch family when we blended our six kids.

At the height of our happiness, having been married for six months, I was diagnosed with breast cancer. It rocked our world. My whole life I was afraid of following the path of my mum, and here I was in my own crisis wondering if I would die. We then had to sit the kids down and explain to them what was happening. When we told them I was calm, but numb. I felt sick to the stomach, and it burned my heart to be the cause of such distress. My eldest son yelled at me through his tears, "I can't lose you Mum!" The others couldn't speak, instead sitting in silence. The panic settled in the air as we were collectively paralysed.

How could I be so happy and yet this big thing be happening to me?

Amongst the chaos and trauma, I learned why.

On the surface I lived a joyful and seemingly happy life. but old stories, patterns and traumas were still running the show in my subconscious. I had immersed in a little of the work needed but I was in no way finished or healed.

I made the decision that it was no longer enough to be surviving, I wanted to thrive. I learnt more about myself than ever before, and I allowed myself to feel it all. The ugliness, the truth, and the pain of all I was holding on to.

I learnt to let it go and love myself.

I empowered myself to grow, to be my most beautiful self in my rawness and to alchemise fear.

I stopped pushing, striving, and forcing, and allowed myself to instead be still, silent, and slow. I found a peace I had never known before.

It is through this place of calm I discovered my passion.

After the light bulb moment of realising my life could have been different many years before, that burning feeling of purpose arose to teach other women how they can empower themselves and give themselves permission to heal.

I studied a Diploma of Psychology formally, at university, and then Life Coaching. I researched, and I created.

Since 2017 I have been working with women all over the world as a coach and therapist. Nothing gives me greater fulfilment than gifting the tools to help women create an environment where they have the power to achieve their own happiness and success.

We are reminded in life every day that empowered women are a force like no other. Women such as those in leadership roles and politics, healers, coaches, therapists, creatives, speakers, and business owners all have one thing in common; they are trailblazers.

We are the changemakers, and our children need us to teach them how to follow us in creating a future that is fueled with love. Our future generations need our help, now, to show them it is possible to be truly happy in the present, so in time it will be our turn to learn from them.

We begin with small steps for ourselves, and on the grand scale we must be role models in sharing our stories of creating happiness.

Embodying self-love, self-acceptance and self-compassion gives us the strength to let go of victimhood and allows us instead to stand in our truth.

It's not about being fierce and fighting your way through. You can take this path if you wish, but you will find yourself exhausted and disillusioned, as I did. This is where I can help.

I'm suggesting we begin here.

This book is filled with daily teachings and are a collection of my writings over several years. The more aware you allow yourself to become of your thoughts, feelings, and behaviours the more you will understand how to live your happiest life. You may find some themes will repeat. This is deliberate, it's one of the ways the human brain learns new information. I am not sharing professional or medical advice, nor do I profess my way is the only way. This book is intended as a lifestyle guide only and invites you to consider how you can take action for yourself.

The illustrations scattered throughout the book are my sketches. They are what I call *meditative drawing* and take me to a place of pure joy. I was inspired by a friend who draws to connect with peace. My drawings are not particularly pretty, or exceptionally talented (not like my professional artist husband!), but they hold a beauty in them that instantly helps me feel joyful when I look at them. Maybe you'd like to try it too.

You may not realise it yet, but you absolutely have the power within yourself to create whatever life you want. Joy, peace, love, success, health, and happiness can become your everyday experience.

Owning who you are right now and creating change is glorious.

Glorious because of the richness of life's experiences that will take you to the next level.

Glorious because of the depths of understanding you will reach about yourself and your world.

Glorious because of the wonder you will embrace when waking each day to the excitement of possibilities that await.

Glorious because of the soul filling connections you will create with other powerful humans who love you for all you are.

And, glorious because of the knowing you've attracted it all, after you made the decision to take back control of your life.

Oh, how glorious is such a responsibility when you transform your pain into a life of happiness.

INTENTION

Intention is a driving force towards changing and achieving anything in your life.

Have you ever noticed when you set your mind on a goal, you will often feel motivated with everything falling into place to accomplish it?

Empowering yourself is no different. It's about shifting your focus from the external to the internal. Come home to you, who you want to be and how you want to feel.

Incorporating daily intentions will help you set the wheels in motion, gain momentum, and teach your brain to focus on what you want, rather than ruminating about what you don't want. It will help transform your mindset to be one of self-worth and self-belief.

The purpose of this book is for you to open to a different page every morning and discover what inspiration reveals itself to you. (I don't believe there is ever anything random by the way!)

You will notice under each teaching there is a section for you to commit to setting your own intention for each day. This is your opportunity to immerse in focusing on all you desire. This is where magic happens.

Use this book as a tool for self-empowerment, to create the changes you want to live your happiest life.

Given that you have it in your hands and are reading this means you've already begun. (Also not random!)

It is my big intention to create change in the world – through one beautiful woman at a time. She who takes responsibility for her life, transforms how she interacts as her goddess self and creates a ripple effect around her. Imagine the existence of humanness that many likeminded women can create.

The symbol on the front cover is the representation of my intention for this book. It is programmed with an invocation I'm sending out to the world.

"Dear one, embrace your vulnerability and be open to a new level of enlightened wholeness. Embody peace, love, and grace as you call in your true nature of happiness."

Here's to your magical, glorious rise.

WHERE ARE YOU NOW?

Let's get real for a moment.

How much joy and happiness do you currently experience in your life, and how is it possible to determine the answer?

There is a tangible way for you to connect with how you currently feel.

Grab a pen and paper and follow the exercise below.

The Emotional Scale

This practice will help you measure your levels of emotion as your starting point. All it requires is for you to take glorious responsibility to be honest with yourself.

Leave any judgement behind at the train station with a no return ticket and take the shuttle to self-awareness! Nothing you come up with is wrong, it just *is*, and you need to know this information to be able to create change.

Close your eyes, get present with your body, and tune into your surroundings. What are you sitting or lying on? Are you comfortable? Do a quick scan of your body from the top of your head down to your toes and consciously relax your muscles. What do you hear? What do you feel?

Place one hand on your belly, and the other on your heart. Take a deep breath as you count to four expanding your belly as much as possible. Hold your breath for the count of four, breathe out to the count of four and hold for the count of four. Repeat several times. This is called *box breathing*. Once you are feeling relaxed you are ready to follow on.

Below is a table of emotions. Read each emotion and focus on it for a few seconds to connect with it in your body.

Think of a number between 0 and 10 to measure the intensity of the emotion, 0 being the least and 10 being the highest. The first number you think of is the truest – it will come from your subconscious. Don't over think it or change it out of concern for how it looks. Remember the judgement?

Complete the scale for each of the emotions and record them on the table.

	The Emotional Scale			
	Date:	Date:	Date:	Date:
Emotion	0......10	0......10	0......10	0......10
Sadness				
Dread				
Hopelessness				
Calm				
Excitement				
Happiness				

Use this template to repeat the exercise every couple of months to check in with yourself and track your progress.

Would you like those numbers to change?

Set yourself an *intention* to aim for a new (realistic) score and set a date in your calendar for the next check in. Eight weeks is the recommended interval. Avoid putting pressure on yourself by inflating future numbers. This could leave you feeling disappointed and self-critical. Embrace self-acceptance and self-compassion through this process and allow yourself to be honest. For example, maybe your level of happiness is currently at a 5. You could set an intention to be at 7 when you do the exercise next.

Measuring your emotions will help you know if you are on the track to wellbeing and happiness or if maybe you could benefit from some support.

Please remember, even if your scores are confronting, they are not wrong, and you are not less than. This is simply your starting point, and you have much to look forward to from here.

"To live your most authentic, bone breathing, happiest life means to take hold of your own truth in your hands where it is safe and warm. See it like you've never seen it before and cherish it like the precious gem of transformation that it is."

Ali Williams

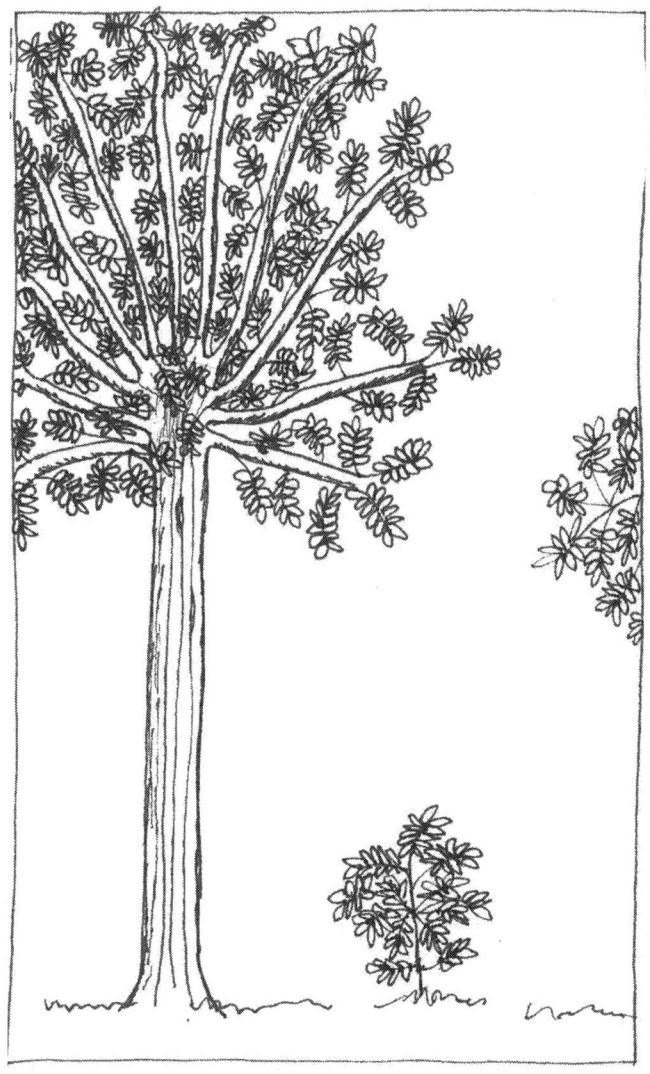

Whatever you are going through is never for nothing.

All you're experiencing serves its purpose for your growth and expansion.

You have an opportunity to make a choice to be the victim, or the alchemist.

The victim feels all the feels but remains stuck in blaming others while waiting for external forces to come to the rescue.

The alchemist feels all the feels but takes responsibility. They seek the learning and draw on inner knowing while stepping up to move through the emotions and create their own transformation.

Be the alchemist.

Intention: Today, I will ....

How you were soothed (or not) as a child has a direct impact on your adult relationships.

To build a wall and avoid letting people in is a survival mode response that may be hard wired from your experiences when you were younger.

Maybe you struggle to trust people, or maybe you recognise that behaviour in others.

It's not your fault, it's how you've adapted to feel safe. It's a protective mechanism from the fear of being disappointed.

It doesn't have to remain that way.

Fear based behaviour can be worked through.

If you recognise this in yourself and want to change it, you can.

Awareness is the first step.

Intention: Today, I will ....

Ever jumped down someone's throat only to wish you could back pedal?

The guilt that rises can be consuming.

When you're in a constant state of stress, you are in a repeating pattern of fight or flight which is the body's response to thoughts and feelings of threat.

When your nervous system is on such high alert and in defence mode you may misread other people's cues. You may interpret other people's behaviour as a personal attack and become reactive.

If you have been in that state of stress chronically, due to situations such as unresolved trauma and adversity, your brain forms thought patterns that reinforce reaction.

Through awareness and active transformation your super charged reactions can change to be more rational and reasonable responses.

This one mindset shift is life changing. It's worth considering.

Intention: Today, I will ....

You can be a goddess-like spiritual being, be zen af *and* watch Netflix!

Whatever works for you is perfect.

You don't have to do life like anyone else.

Intention: Today, I will ....

You can choose to be dissatisfied, or you can choose to be grateful.

Both require emotional energy, but the outcomes are completely different.

Intention: Today, I will ....

You are receiving inspiration and ideas all the time in your thoughts.

Every time you think of something you would like to do it is an opportunity for a new experience.

Embrace them all and open your world to endless possibilities.

You never know where they may lead you.

Intention: Today, I will ....

At times, we all focus on how we look.

Is our makeup perfect? Are we wearing the right outfit? Is our hair looking beautiful for the occasion?

There is nothing wrong with that, we all feel fabulous when we are looking gorgeous. But we are also much more than that.

The beauty we radiate out into the world is from within.

When you are beautiful on the outside, people *see* that. And most often only that.

When you are beautiful on the inside, people *feel* that. You connect with others in a way that only those who are open to receiving love can appreciate.

Be your true self, be your own kind of beautiful and share that with others.

Intention: Today, I will ....

Love yourself enough to not react to other people's behaviour.

Love yourself enough to remember that how someone behaves towards you is not your concern.

How you react is all you need to focus on.

It takes time to change such behaviour, but it is possible through being aware of your choices to do things differently.

Intention: Today, I will ....

Spend time imagining yourself as who you wish to be, and all that you wish to achieve.

Let go of all the inner criticism for all you are not.

The mind always has a way of searching for possibilities to bring about what you believe.

So, change it up, and imagine all the magic.

Intention: Today, I will ....

If you ever think you aren't strong enough, think of everything you have already survived, grown through, and achieved.

Really quite amazing, aren't you?

Intention: Today, I will ....

"It is only when you take responsibility for your life that you discover how truly powerful you are."

Allanah Hunt

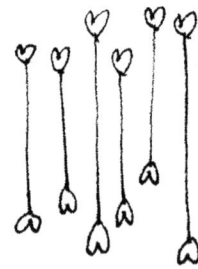

Remember to stop every now and then, close your eyes, put your hands on your heart and take three deep loving breaths.

Smile, and appreciate the little things in your day.

Intention: Today, I will ....

It's a bright lippy and sexy knickers kinda day today!

How long have they been in the drawer? Get them out and wear them just because.

If you don't own any, buy yourself some. No one needs to know, but you will feel damn fine, and everyone will notice your powerful inner goddess radiating out into the world.

Intention: Today, I will ....

Working on yourself is often uncomfortable.

Familiar past behaviours will hold fast.

There may be suffering in the release.

Your transformation in the discomfort will create the true nature of enlightenment.

Intention: Today, I will ....

Share your smile with the world today.

Whatever is happening around you, just turn the corners of your mouth up to stimulate the production of happy hormones.

You will feel more joyful, and it could just change someone else's day.

What a gift.

Intention: Today, I will ....

Today, be your own superhero.

Put your cape on, and your tights, and aim for the stars!

It doesn't matter if others cheer you on or not.

What matters is that you completely believe in yourself and can stand in the face of fear and doubt and ninja chop those villains into a crumpled heap on the ground!

Just for today anyway.

Intention: Today, I will ....

Take a few moments during your day to stop and take three deep belly breaths.

Love yourself enough to accept that you cannot control or change some situations, and it may serve you best to surrender.

Today, be aware of your reactions and emotions. Be your own observer without criticism.

Nothing stays the same. Ever. Empower yourself now to let go and choose not to suffer.

Take a step towards inner peace.

Intention: Today, I will ....

Do you have human angels in your life?

How fortunate we are to have the special bond of connection and friendship.

To have those people who love us unconditionally and accept all we are.

To hold us when we cry and cheer the loudest when celebrating our achievements.

To hear their words of reassurance when we feel fear and doubt.

Never judging, only ever encouraging.

Celebrate those amazing people and remember how grateful you are.

Send a message of love to someone today. Someone who has been there for you through it all. Let them know you appreciate them.

Intention: Today, I will ....

Loving yourself enough to embrace who you are will create your own path towards the future.

Do not minimise your authenticity to fit in with someone else's expectations for the sake of external acceptance.

Never compromise your goddess.

Amazing people will be attracted to you, and they will be all accepting.

Life has so much more meaning with genuine, soul nurturing friendships and connections.

And you are so worth it.

Intention: Today, I will ....

However you give love to others is an indication of the love you feel for yourself.

Remember not to give all of yourself to the point of having nothing left in your own tank.

You come first. Period.

Love yourself first to be able to love others through nurture, support, and service.

What you give, will come back.

Intention: Today, I will ....

Where are you on the list of things you love?

Most of us put ourselves after our partners, children, and friends.

We often feel that caring for everyone else before ourselves will be fulfilling. And it can be, but even more so when you prioritise yourself first.

Love yourself enough to be on the top of your list for wellbeing and happiness.

Show yourself as much kindness and compassion as you do for the special people in your life.

Through self-love, you will effortlessly create more time, space, and energy for others without sacrificing joy and suffering the heaviness of obligation.

Intention: Today, I will ....

"Above all, be the heroine of your life, not the victim."

Nora Ephron

There's a saying, "In a society that profits from your self-doubt, liking yourself is a rebellious act!"

Let's be rebels! Let's level up how we feel about ourselves and create huge change in this world.

It starts with each of us holding our own happiness in our hands and hearts.

Intention: Today, I will ....

Take '5' today. Just for yourself.

Take a few slow, deep breaths.

Stand barefoot on the grass.

Meditate.

Do whatever you can to give your nervous system a break.

Let go of the week that has been so far.

Relax, so your body can heal itself from the inside.

Feeling calm is one way to slow down your nervous system and give it a break from fight or flight and excess cortisol production that may be harmful to our health.

Your internal body is a powerful force that you must take responsibility for healing and nurturing to reach your wholeness of happiness.

Intention: Today, I will ....

Have you ever been told you have your head in the clouds?

Or maybe when you share your dreams with someone, they squash them and complain that it's just not reality?

Dream.

Imagine, visualise, and picture yourself doing things beyond your wildest imagination.

What is reality anyway? You woke up today. That in itself is completely extraordinary.

Dream of unicorns and magic.

Who knows what amazing things you could achieve and experience.

You deserve it, after all.

Intention: Today, I will ....

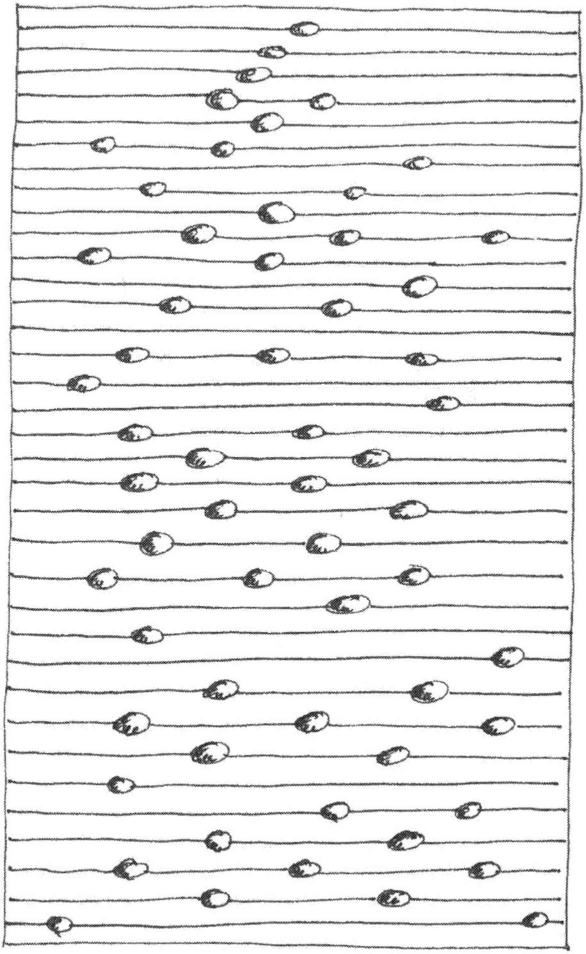

If you want more peace, love, joy, and success in your life, you need to focus on peace, love, and joy.

Success will follow.

Intention: Today, I will ....∴.............................

Our path towards happiness is often challenging.

There are always plenty of lessons and curveballs along the way, but we keep getting back on the bike regardless.

You have a choice how you view those experiences.

While it can't be rainbows and butterflies all the time, you can acknowledge how you feel, put self-care into practice, and know you will get through.

Embrace it all through grace and the understanding that your happiness is a magical collection of experiences that call you to rise to new levels of wisdom, soul growth and humanness.

Intention: Today, I will ....

We as mums, aunts, sisters, step-mums, colleagues, friends, and anyone else who is ever connected to young people, have the knowledge and experience to raise beautiful, powerful, and amazing children.

We have the opportunity to teach them to do things differently than we did.

We can teach them how to accept and love themselves, and not compare themselves with others. We can teach them they are good enough, no matter what.

They need to hear they are beautiful, brave, and strong.

There is no denying they can be hard work some days as they try to navigate their way through finding their identity and where they fit in this world. But they themselves must figure it out. They need to make mistakes, with our support and guidance.

Hold them. For longer.

Encourage them to question. Encourage them to be brave.

Let them believe they can give something a go. Don't tell them they can't or won't. Tell them they can.

Let them dream big and smile when they share their thoughts about the future.

Tell them it doesn't matter what others think, even when they cry tears over that text message or conversation. Teach them to not take other people's behaviour personally and teach them to not make assumptions.

Teach them also, to take responsibility for their happiness and to not give their power away to others.

Remind them to always trust in themselves, what they feel, and what they dream.

Our children are our future, let's invest in them.

Intention: Today, I will ....

Hug your babies a little bit longer when you say good night and good morning.

Kiss your special people.

Smile at everyone today.

Stand with your face to the sun, just for a few minutes and breathe deep.

Feel the grass or sand with your bare feet and drink your coffee slowly.

Put aside some of those jobs you must do today, for they can wait until tomorrow.

Stop, look, and listen. Even for a few minutes.

Be mindful and notice what is happening around you.

What do you see and hear?

There is joy in the little moments, and in the joy there is power.

Intention: Today, I will ....

SIYAGRUVA
A series of novels for South African teens

HIGH HEELS AND HIJACK

NIBOR NALAM

Of course, Shelley knows better than her mother! Or does she? Tonight is a big night for her – but it could end in disaster. Nothing gets Thabiso down! But what happens the night he's not in his wheelchair? Can his wits pull him through?

'Young people deal with hate, jealousy, friendship and danger every day – and comedy!'
– A reader

SIYAGRUVA

A series of novels for South African teens

DIVINE DUMP DANCER

RUSSELL H KASCHULA

From the dumps to divining, from despair to dancing! This happens to Mncedisi when he and his mother come to the city. Some people are called to fulfil their role and responsibility to family and community. Could you travel the journey Mncedisi has to?

'He's not a quitter, he has courage and strength – and he's a great dancer!'
– A reader

SIYAGRUVA
A series of novels for South African teens

BREAKING OUT

COLLEEN MOROUKIAN

Rashaad is going through a tough time. His religion, his culture, even his sexuality ... who and what is he? Samantha and her friend Nolwazi are playing a dangerous double-game with their parents. Into their lives comes The Siyagruva Scene – and things start happening!

'Rashaad faces reality and becomes a man. Samantha learns to think for herself.'
– A reader

'Darn right, Thabs! They look like champions, right now. Like winners through and through!'

'Come, guys, come, come, come! You're next! Get over here!'

Zadie has just enough time to give him a special wink and a squeeze of the hand as they rush to the tunnel that leads to the dance floor. The music draws them out onto the floor. It's a tango. Zadie and Regan dance with all the passion their two young bodies can find. They're full of fire. They almost seem to run ahead of the music, which has to hurry to keep up with them. This feels good and right. The music throbs. This dancing gives them a real rush.

'Does them good to have a bit of a bad time, doesn't it?' says Thabiso to Raymondo, who is sitting with him and staring in surprise at how brilliantly they are dancing.

Raymondo laughs out loud.

he is. He was always just her dance partner. A bit too short for her liking, but a good mover on the dance floor.

'Zadie, I learnt something this week too.'

Softly, he tells her about all his troubles. He makes her see that it was because of her that he had been so messed up.

He laughs a little.

'I can see you're, like, surprised, Zee! Don't worry, my girl! You aren't the only one who's surprised. Me too, baby. Me too! Me and Zadie! I always thought we were just partners on the floor. This has made me see something else, girl. I see that ... hey, I don't really know ... maybe, you're more special ...'

And that's as far as he can go because suddenly there's a rush of wheels and Thabiso is there.

It's not easy for her, but she decides she must tell him the truth. Well, part of it, actually. She doesn't need to tell him about her dreams, does she? Or just how much she'd fancied Bernard.

Quickly she tells him a little about her week. She can't look him straight in the eyes. She keeps her eyes on the other dancers on the floor and taps her feet as she watches.

Regan takes both her hands in his. He makes her look straight at him.

'Zadie,' he says softly. She is surprised. Regan isn't usually so gentle. He's usually full of jokes and stuff. Not holding her hands and looking into her eyes, that's for sure. She wants to laugh suddenly. This was how it should have been with Bernard. She'd never thought of Regan being like this. Never noticed even how good-looking

wheeled himself away. Before he went, though, he had nodded his head to Zadie, so she would know to lean over to listen to his whispered words.

'Sort it out, man!' he had whispered to her. It sounds like an order and it is. When Thabiso bosses, they listen. It's hard to say 'No' to a guy in a wheelchair who acts so much like he's not in one, even though he used to be a great soccer player before his accident. Zadie nods her head at him. She knows she must make it right with Regan, but there's been such a rush to get here and get changed and everything. And Regan has seemed so cross. She knows she has messed him around by not coming to dance class. She also knows she had been planning to mess him around even more. Until she got scared of that Bernard.

is looking very pale and she keeps cracking her knuckles and looking at Regan out of the corner of her eye. She wants to say something, that's clear.

It's coming round to their turn and they are still so tense with each other. They're never going to be able to get it right, Regan is sure. It's a sport, okay, but it's still two people dancing like one. You must look beautiful when you dance and, at the same time, you must be out there meaning to win. Your face is also in the contest: it must look happy, as if you are enjoying yourself. Right now, everything still feels wrong.

Suddenly, Regan feels a little hand sliding softly into his. He nearly makes a noise he can't help. But he keeps holding it and looks down at Zadie's soft hand. While he was feeling sorry for himself, Thabiso quietly

Chapter 12

It's dance time!

As they sit at the edge of the dance floor, Regan and Zadie take little looks at each other. Thabiso is sitting between them in his wheelchair, leaning forward and nodding his head to the beat, so they can't really see each other properly.

The competition has already begun. Zadie

dumb girl. He's messed up. He's fixed up the mess. Hey, if he'd really meant to have the spliff, there was last night, wasn't there? And if he'd been a hard-core druggie he wouldn't have come anywhere near school today, would he? And now, hardest of all, he's told some little kid all this stuff. Him! Georgie! Regan trusted him!

And Georgie knows he won't let Regan down.

'It's okay, man!' he says.

'It's okay, dude,' he adds.

'Cool! Dance rules! You're no fool! Thanks, dude.'

With a high five, Regan is off. It's been a tough day. Will Zadie be there tomorrow?

Regan is looking at him, sadly, and cracking his knuckles.

Georgie thinks about everything Regan has done in the last few hours. Actually, a lot of it was pretty cool. That thing of making him sit on the loo with his pants down – *Jeez!* – that was risky.

Ja, but look! He was the one who planted the stuff on Georgie in the first place.

What kind of hero does that?

Regan is chewing on the side of his nail and he's stopped kicking and clicking. Sitting there, he looks just like a kid himself.

Georgie suddenly knows that Regan is ... well ... ordinary. He knows that it's not clever to make like someone ordinary is someone great. But ... and this is interesting ... he also knows that Regan really is great. Look at all he's done. He's cared about some

And while he raps he kicks his heels against the kerb, making the rhythm stronger. Soon he's clicking his fingers too and his eyes are closed.

Suddenly he stops. Checks Georgie out. How's he doing? What's Georgie thinking? This is important to him.

Georgie is quiet.

He sits there, still, a bit longer – and quiet.

He looks at Regan. His hero.

What is a hero, actually?

This guy, this Regan, he's just ordinary.

Georgie half laughs. That's funny, really.

It feels a bit better. Ever since he read that the guy who played Superman broke his neck or something, he's had a bit of a funny feeling about heroes. Now the guy, that Christopher Reeve, is a new kind of super-hero – fighting to stay alive and all.

He sighs again.

'It's a girl, man. *Ja*, surprises me too, *ek sê*,' he adds.

Slowly, he tells Georgie. Talks about Zadie, about getting cross, about buying the spliff being just something stupid, about how he wasn't going to buy it, wasn't going to use it. He tells about all the long months of getting off drugs, getting out of the gang, leaving his worst friends from the old gang.

'It's all the dancing, man. As soon as I got into it and we won that competition, then it was all ... I can't say ... it was like,

'Hey boy, don'cha see,
Life's okay and it's waiting for me.
Can't you think and don't you know,
There's new places out there to go.'

Chapter 11

After school, Regan and Georgie walk away around the corner and sit on the kerbside. Regan sighs and kicks his heel against the kerb a bit. Georgie is looking at him. He's got to go on.

'Georgie, I made a mistake.'

He looks at Georgie carefully. Is he believing him?

out of it' before they really force him in. They reckon they're the Acid Boys, not the Asthma Boys.

Now this thing with Regan is making his chest feel all tight. Right now he can hear the air wheezing and feel the drag in his chest. He sighs when he thinks of the long night ahead.

Regan waits till the dogs are out of the toilets and heading off to the bins near the gates. Then he walks over to Georgie again.

'See you after school, bru,

Tell you all, and tell you true.'

And he winks his usual friendly wink.

Georgie feels better. When Regan is doing one of his silly rhymes, then he's okay. And when Regan's okay, then Georgie's okay.

deserves it. Number two: Is Georgie safe? Will he keep quiet?

Georgie doesn't know what he wants. Part of him wants to run away and never come back. He wants to cry even – like run to his mommy. What is all this about? All these months he thought Regan was great! Regan's such a clean good guy. He's cool and he's funny, and he's a guy who used to be part of a real-life gang. But he got out. He got out of a gang! Man!

Georgie wants to know how Regan could do this. He really needs to know because, to him, getting out of a gang is like magic.

Georgie's brother is stuck in the Acid Boys gang and they have been trying to get him in too. So far, it's been okay. Georgie has asthma. He goes to the hospital so often that the gang has decided to let him 'grow out, and then you lose teachers, and then the school is on the way down – all the way to the bottom. He'd rather just keep everything the way it is.

Regan and Georgie look at one another. They don't need to be asked a second time. Regan is nearest the door and he's out of there so fast. Georgie is right behind him. Once they are out, though, they nearly turn round and run straight back in. They run right out into the place where 700 kids are staring at them. There's a loud shout when the two guys go out. Kids laugh and joke. The jokes are rude ones about guys in loos and about jail and about druggies.

Regan just wants to disappear into the crowd so they will all stop looking at him and mocking him. But he knows he has to talk to Georgie. Number one: Georgie

Chapter 10

'Get out, you guys! Go on!'

Mr Cupido is worried. He hopes he can get these two guys out of there. The sooner the dogs are back in their trailer, the happier he will be. He does not want any bad publicity for his school. All it takes is one small thing and it's all over the papers. Next thing, the parents are taking their children

it right into his eye if she needed to? How could that happy face be the face of a terrified girl who was going to fight like a cage of tigers if he tried anything on her? Let him just try!

He sits still. He's thinking.

'We can meet tomorrow, Bernie. I'll get you after school.'

He waits some more.

She feels the sharp nailfile in her hand.

'Don't call me Bernie, woman. I don't like that. I don't like being called Bernie, you hear?'

And he looks mad. Really mad.

she pushes her hand through her hair and shouts again. Man, this is irritating. What's she up to?

'Bernard! Oh, man! Look what you made me do, man!'

'What? What?' he asks, confused.

'My hair, man – I was supposed to go to my cousin's house to get it done this afternoon. It's the competition this Saturday, man. My hair's a mess!'

While she talks, she pulls at her hair to make it look as bad as possible.

She leans over and shakes his arm.

'Quick! Quick! If we hurry, we can just make it and you can get a load of passengers at Wynberg. Go, Bernard! Go, man, go!'

She looks at him with a happy, bright face.

How would he guess that she was feeling in her bag for her nailfile, so she could stab sweaty little big-deal guy!

The music makes her strong. It gives her a rhythm and an idea about how she could save herself.

Leaning forward, Zadie pushes in the Black Noise tape Bernard likes so much.

She wriggles a little and looks at him. She laughs loudly. She's doing all she can to seem like an older woman. She knows that she mustn't look like an easy lay for Bernard – like an eager little girl.

She knows she must act fast while the sexy mood he's been working on is broken. She looks at her watch and shouts, 'Look at the time, man!'

He sits up, surprised.

'It's your busy time, Bernard! Just look at it, man!'

As he stares in surprise at this new girl,

into Zadie's body. Her body starts to move along with the sound. This was what Bernard wanted, after all – a throbbing, wild chick. He's just about to reach his hand right up her skirt when she jumps her strong body along the seat to far over under the passenger window.

The beat of the music gives her strength – suddenly she's Zadie the dancer queen, Zadie the winner, Zadie the one who was really making it in a way her two older sisters hadn't. She is Zadie, the one her little sister looks up to. Zadie, the one who trains groups for 21st parties, showing them all the *passies* and earning some good money, which she could use to help buy a few things around the house. She is also Zadie the virgin. And this baby isn't going to stop being a virgin just for this small-eyed, like this one. It makes the whole thing a lot more fun.

He teases her. 'It's okay, baby, I just want a little rest and a little chance to talk. Chance to have a smoke and all.'

Bernard leans over and turns on the radio. He turns the radio up loud and lies back, clicking the fingers of his right hand. He puts his left hand on Zadie's left knee. His arm lies across her body and his elbow is rubbing against her left breast.

Zadie stares at Bernard's hand. She feels the rub-rub-rub of his elbow on her breast. His eyes are closed, but his body is tense.

This doesn't seem like a little talk. And he's not looking deep into her eyes like in the movies. He doesn't even know her whole name or anything about her, it seems.

The beat-beat-beat of the drums gets right

She puts her head on Bernard's shoulder, just for a moment. He grabs her hard across the shoulders and pulls her over for a kiss. It's so wild and hard that it even seems to hurt. Zadie is confused. Is this the gentle, kind kiss she has had so many times in her dreams?

She pulls back. The taste of Bernard is in her mouth. Why did he stick his tongue in her mouth? *Sis!* She can taste some wine, she thinks. Or is it only cough mixture? Where are they, anyway? She looks at Bernard. Is he laughing at her?

Bernard laughs aloud. He likes this business. It's fun in a lovely, sick way and he's giving up a good run, with lots of passengers, at peak time, for the fun of it. He likes it when they're a little scared. He likes it when they're young and not too rich – just

Chapter 9

Halfway through Bernard's sixth trip back from Mitchell's Plain, he takes a quick left. After a while, he heads the taxi down a sand road and then straight into a clearing among some wattle trees.

For the first little part of the trip, Zadie is laughing.

'What you doing, Bernard? Careful, man!'

is looking at him. Georgie opens his mouth to speak. He closes it again.

Then, suddenly, Georgie turns round and flushes the toilet.

Right behind the men and the dogs are Mr Cupido and Mr Arendse, the Grade 12 English teacher. Seems like everybody is looking at Regan.

'What's going on here?' Mr Cupido shouts. 'Why aren't you outside with the rest?'

Regan can't talk. He can't think.

The dogs have stopped – one standing in front of Georgie and one in front of Regan. They're barking and barking.

What does it mean? Regan wishes he knew. Are they just barking because they are there or is this their special drugs bark? Will the police know he's lying if he says he's just there to use the toilet? What will Georgie say?

'*Kom, jong!*' shouts the biggest cop.

Regan is quiet. Across the room, Georgie

He pulls the chain quickly. For a few desperate moments, the little piece of paper just goes round and round the toilet bowl. At last, after what seems like ages, it is sucked away. Has all the stuff gone?

Regan pulls down Georgie's pants and pushes him down to sit on the toilet seat.

'Flush it again!' he hisses at Georgie. 'Flush it, man!'

Then Regan rushes to the urinal on the other side of the room.

A moment later, the dogs and their handlers charge into the toilet area. The place is full of noise, men, dogs and fear. Regan forces himself to pee and then turns round carefully. He can just see Georgie jumping up and zipping his pants. Georgie is staring at Regan. He really needs to know what this is all about.

Chapter 8

Georgie and Regan listen to the dogs barking outside. They listen to the excited noises of the kids out there. They look at each other. The sounds are coming nearer.

Suddenly, Regan dives forward and grabs the little wad of paper and spliff from Georgie's pocket. He throws it in the second toilet because it's the only one that usually flushes.

look cool. He mustn't think she's easy.

'Get in, baby.'

It's him!

Zadie quickly checks her hair with a little pat of her hand.

She doesn't mind that her skirt is right up as she gets onto the high seat next to the driver.

She likes the way Bernard nudges her and then kisses her ear.

She likes the way he revs the engine and drives off fast.

She just wishes Janine was there on the pavement so she could give her a cheeky wave as they drive off. Instead, she smiles at Bernard and moves a little closer to him.

Chapter 7

A few kilometres away, Zadie is walking along the road. Her skirt is rolled up as far as it can go. Her make-up is now on. She's written her test, waved a secret goodbye to the worried Janine, and now she's off.

Before she can even reach the rank, though, a taxi slows down next to her. She tries hard not to look up. She wants to

They stand there breathing heavily and stare at one another.

Regan can't think what to say.

'What, man? What?' asks Georgie.

Georgie is bewildered. If Regan is a hero, then this is okay. But what's going on? And he really wants to see those dogs in action. He's been thinking about them almost all week. He loves the idea that a dog can track down a little speck of dope.

Regan stares at Georgie some more. Suddenly he speaks. 'Do you want to start dance class, Georgie? It's cool, man! How about it?'

He's wondering if he can try to pat the guy on the shoulder again and get the spliff out that way somehow.

Georgie stares blankly at him. Is Regan completely mad?

Regan runs around the back of the crowd and pulls Georgie through some kids.

Georgie looks up in surprise and yells, 'Hey, man!' when he's grabbed. He stops when he sees that it's Regan. But why's he looking so mad? And why's he grabbing him like this?

Regan keeps a tight grip on Georgie's arm and starts to hustle him off towards the boys' loos. There are a few stares and one or two guys even whistle. What are Regan and Georgie up to?

As they jog along, Regan is full of panic again. How can he grab the spliff? Georgie will think he's grabbing like a *moffie*. He'll fight and then they'll get caught anyway.

They run into the stinking toilets at last and Georgie breaks loose.

'What you doing, man?'

and even heard about jobs in the police force.

Everybody's heard this, except Regan. Regan can't hear anything except a voice in his mind, like at the dance competitions. But the voice isn't saying: 'And the winners are ... Couple Number 12, Regan Appollis and Zadie Hendricks,' as it usually does. The voice is saying: 'And the loser is ... Regan,' and again: 'The loser is Regan.'

Now it's time for the dogs to run and sniff. All the kids have to stand right back and stand still.

The school is very excited. The panting dogs pull on their chains.

Suddenly, the magic spell around Regan breaks. He sees Georgie. Georgie's young face is full of childish excitement. He's happy and just a child. What has Regan done?

Chapter 6

Regan's school seems to be full of police and dogs, even though there are only two dogs.

They have finished the talk about bombs and about pipe bombs and about homemade bombs. They've heard about how you must call the police if you think there's trouble. They've heard how you mustn't take dope,

Zadie's mother is a domestic worker with four daughters and no money. Two of them are still at school. They all live in one room at her mommy's work.

Zadie has been doing so well with her dancing and all her fame and all. Now what's she up to these last few weeks? It looks like she's heading for trouble and Janine, for one, wants to get in there and help her if she can.

Janine waits restlessly, while Zadie quickly smudges off her make-up and gets her stuff.

When they get to the class, Miss thinks the little bit of blue around Zadie's eyes is because she feels a bit off. What a joke!

'There's always tomorrow,' Zadie thinks as she starts to read the test.

'Sadie!' There's another call. 'It's me – Janine. Open up, man!'

Zadie sighs and opens the door quickly.

Janine takes in Zadie's make-up. She grins at her. But then she sees that Zadie is not in the mood for jokes. She explains quickly.

'Sadie, man, you must come quickly! There's a surprise test and Miss knows you were at school just now. If you don't get to class quickly, you'll get into trouble for sure. I told her you had tummy gripes and she said I must come get you. Come on, man. You must. You know you're already in trouble with all the homework you didn't do the other day! And you stayed at home last week that one day!'

Janine's face is very worried. She likes Zadie and would have lots to talk to Regan about if she only knew how worried he was.

others for a change. She wants to surprise him. She can see herself, walking across the taxi rank, swinging her dancer's hips, acting shocked when all the other guys whistle, looking cool when the other taxi-*tjerries* look her up and down and check to see if their men are really eyeing this one.

She looks in her bag for her make-up and waits impatiently for the other girls all to leave for class. They take ages.

At last it is quiet. She takes out her make-up and her little mirror and starts with her eyes.

She hears footsteps coming.

She sits dead still.

'Sadie! Sadie!' Someone is whispering her new cool name as loudly as she can.

She panics.

Who is it?

Chapter 5

Across a few suburbs, Zadie is sitting on a broken toilet seat, waiting for everybody to go back to class at the end of the interval. She hasn't been able to think straight all day. Keeps drawing hearts with Bernard's name in them. 'Bernard September'. 'BS'.

She's planning to bunk out of school early so she can get across to Bernard before the

He waves nervously to Regan. 'Come!'

Regan panics. He takes his hand out of his pocket with the little screw of weed in it. His arm goes round Georgie, as if he's saying 'Cheers'. With a quick push, he sticks the stuff into Georgie's pocket.

He sees Georgie's little blush. It's like, 'Hey, I'm friends with the big guy!' Georgie feels great!

Regan doesn't feel great.

He feels like a murderer as he moves off to join old Cupido. He looks miserably at the helluva big guys with the cold eyes who're standing there next to him. He listens to the dogs barking. He sees the little trailer shake as they jump around.

'Morning, sirs.' And then to Mr Cupido, 'Sorry, sir.'

one dog and one cop away from being a criminal.

He feels the small twist of the Rastaman's paper in his pocket.

He sees the police car pulling the little trailer of barking dogs. It drives through the gates of the school while he stands there, glued to the ground.

He breathes fast!

He suddenly remembers that his teacher asked him to do the little welcome speech for these dudes.

What the hell is he supposed to do now?

He sees Mr Cupido, the principal, rushing out of the office to say 'Hello' to the visitors. Old Cupido is a little worried, to tell the truth. What if they find the whole school full of drugs? The sooner they finish, the better he'll feel.

That's why they are on chains. Those dogs can kill a guy for just one *zol* if they haven't had some for a long time. Some of the real druggies haven't even come to school today – they scheme the dogs will just jump on them anyway, even if they're clean for the day!'

Regan's face freezes. If Georgie only took the time to look properly at him, he would see that his hero was white like a whole heap of cocaine.

Of course! The Drug Cops are coming today to give a talk! And they're bringing their dogs!

He knows this. Yesterday he was cool about it. Yesterday he was an ex-druggie. Yesterday he was Mr Clean. Yesterday he was Mr Dance – the guy who'd found a way out.

Now ... he's just one bit of paper and

and Drugs guys?' Georgie calls out when he's still a little way away.

Regan stares blankly.

'What you say?' he asks.

He half remembers something dreadful, but he's not sure what. He feels like someone's walking quietly along behind him in a dark street and is going to jump out soon with a gun or a long quiet knife and murder him.

'The police dogs, Regan! Didn't you know? The police are coming to talk about how to find bombs and all, and about this violence, and they're bringing the dogs to show how they sniff things out. Like anybody would be stupid enough to bring drugs today of all days. *Jus!* Those dogs are vicious, you know. They train them on drugs, you know. They turn the dogs into addicts themselves.

words. Sometimes Regan is not too kind and he uses Georgie to run to the shop to get him something, or to carry his bag, or whatever.

Since he hit the big time with his dancing and started to be clean and to stop drugs (even cigarettes) and so on, he's even seen his mates looking at him like that. Like ... Big Eyes ... like they wish they could also Make It Big. Like they wish they could find something to help them to get out of always doing the same things. Like they wish they could have a future outside this place.

Regan sighs. It's okay, but it's not all great. Being a hero is a bit tough sometimes.

He waves 'Hi' to Georgie, who comes over quickly.

He's ultra-excited today.

'You guys also going to see those Bomb

Chapter 4

Thursday: school. The end of the first interval.

Regan sees Georgie trying to catch his eye. Georgie's in Grade 8 and he thinks Regan is the coolest dude in school. He's always trying to catch his eye, to say 'Hi', to have a little chat – anything. Sometimes Regan is kind to him and slows down for a few

speeds forward to when the taxi empties. Instead of chucking her out so she has to walk home, Bernard drives her home. His strong arms wind around her and he gives her a soft kiss.

'Thanks, babe, you were great today. See you tomorrow, then.'

Zadie wriggles in bed and pulls some sheet away from Monique. She knows she shouldn't keep missing dancing, but she can't go dance tomorrow.

She just has to keep this thing with Bernard going. He's so cool.

And a guy with a car – well, what more could you ask for?

dreaming away. He stuffs it into the bottom of his pocket.

Later that night, when he remembers the dagga for a moment, he's too sleepy to move it to a safer place.

Over on the other side of town, Zadie lies on the mattress she shares with her little sister, Monique. She listens to the hot *tick tick* of the metal roof. She smiles a little while she lies there in the dark.

She's thinking of Bernard.

In her head, she's in a taxi. Up in the front of the taxi are Zadie and Bernard. He's taking little looks at her when he's not too busy with the driving. She's rolled her skirt up as short as it can go. She sticks out her tongue a bit to tease him. She laughs a lot and says very clever, funny, cute things.

Then she dreams the dream faster and

Chapter 3

Regan didn't buy any dagga on the way in to the studio. But he does buy some on the way out.

Once again, Zadie was not there. He's just wasting his time now. No point in trying to dance without a partner. Bloody waste of time.

He buys a few grams from the Rasta, who's

Mncedisi looks up and sees laughing faces looking in through both doors, and he knows he's had it this time.

He nods his head. Laughs. Sighs. How can he save it?

Ha! He steps forward quickly, clicks his heels together and takes Raymondo's hand. He bows over it and gives it a kiss.

'Sorry! *Jammer! Uxolo!* Forgive me, sir. It will not happen again.'

Raymondo snorts. 'Okay, okay, okay! Enough then! Back to your spot, now. As we were.'

Regan laughs and moves on. He's booked the small studio for thirty minutes. Will Zadie be there?

Disi does a little bow and then a salute.

'Yusssir!'

'Well?' asks Raymondo after a while.

'Sir?'

Disi is confused. Raymondo seems to want him to look at something, but all he can see is his own face looking at him from the new mirror on the wall.

Oh no! It can't be! What a fool!

Here he's been doing all his childish old tricks, forgetting – How could he? Is he mad? – their brand new studio mirror! After all this time, at last they have a mirror on the wall of this studio too. Raymondo is dancing away and looking straight into the nice new mirror – and there's dumb, dumb Disi mocking him. And all along, there's Raymondo checking him out and just waiting to catch him.

At last, Disi can't wait any more. He looks up – just a little. Can Raymondo be laughing? Is this true?

Suddenly the whole room is full of giggles and shouts of laughter. Everyone in the room is laughing loudly. And that includes Raymondo.

'Come, my man,' Raymondo says after a long while, taking Disi by the elbow and walking to the front. What can all this mean? Mncedisi tries to smile and look cool again as fast as he can. He needs to win something out of this. He changes his way of walking, so he walks like the Pink Panther. When Raymondo makes him stop, Disi quickly turns around to look at the class and gives a cool kind of wave.

'Hey!' yells Raymondo. 'I'm not finished with you yet, boy!'

when Samantha is in the class and he can enjoy the flash in her eyes and her happy little smile. Sometimes he can use this trick to get her to like him, it seems, and he just loves it.

He stands still. He bows his head and looks like a naughty little child. This usually wins him a break if someone is cross with him. But this time Raymondo is really mad, it seems.

Raymondo shouts again, 'I said get up here, man, right now, this minute!'

Disi walks slowly forward. He keeps his head down. In fact, he's now really sad. He likes Raymondo. He was just playing the fool for a bit. But now Raymondo is standing there with eyes popping and his whole body shaking.

There is a long time of quiet.

dancing room. Raymondo is dancing crossly at the front of the room and shouting a whole lot of things all the time while he dances. The class stands still, watching. Right near the front of the group he can see Mncedisi, who tosses his head as he quietly copies and mocks Raymondo's movements.

While he watches, there is a little sound that goes around the room as more and more of the group see what Mncedisi is up to. Soon they are all watching Disi instead of Raymondo.

Suddenly, there is a terrible growl from Raymondo as he spins around and shouts,

'Get up here, you *mugu*. Who do you think you are, then? Sonya Mayo?'

Disi is confused. How did Raymondo see? He never has before. This is Mncedisi's usual trick. He loves playing the fool, especially

Chapter 2

Once he's in the studio he starts to relax. There are always those two exciting things there – the sounds and the smells. In each of the three studios there's a special set of sounds and rhythms. He's here today to work on the tango a bit more, to get ready for the zone competition on Saturday.

He laughs when he looks in on the jazz-

at him a lot lately. He wonders if they think he's not so cool any more, maybe?

What's that Zadie-babe doing, man?

The taxi stops opposite Shoprite, and Regan picks up his bag and jumps out. He slowly walks across the road, still worrying about Zadie. It seems funny that a guy should need his partner to make him feel good, hey?

As he walks past the Rastaman on the corner, he gets the sweet smell of spliff up his nose. A *zol*, hey. That's what he would have had in the old days. Before all this dancing and this fame, he would have bought some weed and made his own peace.

But that was the old Regan – the gangster guy. The new Regan, the dancing dude, doesn't stop to buy. He walks on to the studio. It's time to dance.

dancer's legs. He also knows that the glue on her newly painted blue-and-gold high heel might not hold her shoe together for more than another week or two.

He sighs and opens his eyes as the taxi hoots and brakes. His dream is over.

He wonders for the hundredth time that day what Zadie is up to. Where is she going off to every day? Why does she keep bunking dance class? She won't even call him back when he tries to get a message to her at the house where her mother works. Something's wrong with Zadie. And it's messing him up too.

He's a bit surprised that he's so messed. He didn't think of Zadie as his *tjerrie*. But since she's been acting funny, he's also not been quite right, has he? He smiles to himself. Silly, hey? He's been seeing his mates looking

Chapter 1

Regan is sitting in a taxi as it races up to the Main Road. But his eyes are closed and, inside his head, it's not Wednesday anymore, but Saturday afternoon – dance time. He can hear the screams of the fans and he can feel Zadie's slim hips twirling under his hands. He knows that her flying, shiny blue satin skirt is showing off her long

First published 2002
Second impression 2005

© New Africa Books (Pty) Ltd
99 Garfield Road
Claremont 7700
South Africa

This book is copyright under the Berne Convention. In terms of the Copyright Act, No. 98 of 1978, no part of this book may be reproduced or transmitted in any form or by any means, electronic or mechanical, including photocopying, recording or by any information storage and retrieval system, without permission in writing from the Publisher.

ISBN: 1-919876-88-X

Series editor: Robin Malan
Copy editor: Sean Fraser
Proof reader: Hilda Hermann
Text design and layout: Jenny Wheeldon
Typesetting: Stacey Gibson
Cover design and layout: Orchard Publishing
Photographs: John Haigh

We acknowledge the encouragement for this project received from Elisabeth Anderson, Head: Centre for the Book.

Origination: House of Colours

Printed and bound in the Republic of South Africa by Shumani Printers.

BRENT LIBRARIES
Please return/renew this item
by the last date shown.
Books may also be renewed by
phone or online.
Tel: 020 8937 3400
On-line **www.brent.gov.uk/libraryservice**

Printed in Great Britain
by Amazon

17816194R00167

When Ali's not working on her mission to create change in the world through one beautiful woman at a time, she enjoys spending time with her family, hanging out at the beach, and catching up with the latest movies. Ali also volunteers at the hospital where she receives treatment, and mentors women experiencing Breast Cancer.

Ali passionately believes that everyone can change their life, even when experiencing trauma and adversity. No matter what the situation, she says, "The darkest times have the potential to create the greatest personal transformation, and there is always an opportunity to seek moments of joy. We start with the tiniest, simplest moments of magic and build from there."

Stay connected with Ali through her free Facebook group for women, *The Self Love Project* at https://www.facebook.com/groups/selfloveprojectwithali

Follow along on Instagram:
@aliwilliamscoachingandtherapy

Email directly: aliwilliamscoaching@gmail.com.au

Receive the newsletter: https://bit.ly/353uBIa

Discover services available:
https://linktr.ee/aliwilliamscoachingandtherapy

ABOUT THE AUTHOR

Ali Williams is a coach and therapist based in Adelaide, South Australia. A farmer's daughter with a preference to be connected to the earth at any opportunity, she believes in a simplistic approach to wellness and healing.

After being diagnosed with Breast Cancer in 2015, Ali embraced the opportunity for awakening and found purpose and passion in teaching others to reconnect with happiness.

Ali launched her business in 2017 after completing a Diploma of Psychology through Charles Darwin University and a Life Coaching Certificate. She works with clients one-to-one and facilitates workshops and courses.

always been filled with joy and have turned out to be awesome humans. I'm proud to call them my children. I hope my legacy will be one that encourages them to continue to give the big things a go in life and be brave.

Another special woman, also named Lisa, a former client, has played a major part in this book being birthed. As I sat in her home one Sunday morning in her art class, she led the group through a meditation. During that moment of peace, I received the very clear download that I needed to create this book. I am grateful for the moment she created in her living room that day when the seed was planted. It is true what they say, "From little things, big things grow."

Most of all, I want to say thank you to my husband, Phil. I started writing at the beginning of my cancer treatment and over time it has grown into a passion. Every step of the way he has told me to, "Go for it!" Phil always has my back, no matter what, and I am blessed to share my life with him. His support lifts me up on the days I don't think I can persevere. We have experienced a lot in life together, and side-by-side, holding hands, we are stronger. He teaches me to be better. As a husband who contemplates what it means for his wife to be living with Metastatic Breast Cancer, he lays his own trauma to rest as he first ensures the rabbit hole doesn't swallow me all the way to doomsday. Admirable, underestimated and underappreciated is the man who is constant and unwavering in his love for me. Thank you, babe, for choosing me.

There were many people who played a part in me being able to learn from Joanne. People I will never be able to repay. Family members, friends, personal mentors, strangers, and friends of friends all generously donated to a fundraising campaign that enabled me to participate in the writing mentorship program. Asking for help on such a large scale made me want to throw up out of fear, but there was a powerful force orchestrating the synchronicities that allowed everything to fall into place. It was one of the most magical experiences in my life.

To my friends, clients and colleagues who have been cheering me on from the sidelines, I thank you for feeling as excited as I do for this book to be introduced to the world. You know who you are. And thank you Jacque for reminding me to connect with my roots and the generations who came before me.

To my bestie, Lou, who has known me since I was 12 years old and gifts me her love and encouragement unconditionally, I am grateful. Lou always reminds me of the value of my work, and the power of my strength, when I need to hear it the most. She is my soul sister. We never run out of words, even after 40 years, and our time is shared talking about the complexities of being human, the rawness of our experiences, and all the amazing wonders in the world. We often marvel at how rare such a friendship as ours is.

To my kids who always say, "That's cool!" when I tell them what I'm up to. They never judge me and are accepting of all that is. They've had a unique upbringing that hasn't

ACKNOWLEDGEMENTS

Over the last five years I have been writing three books. This one happens to be the first, and I'm realising through this process how many people are involved behind the scenes to help pull such a project together.

I have been gifted the privilege of working with many mentors from all over the world in recent years and every one of them has been part of my evolution to end up here with the courage to publish this book. There is a special place in my heart for them and how they have helped me. I would need many pages to list them all, and I fear I would forget someone, but the people I have mentioned below have their essence woven into the words that are by now integrating into your being.

Thank you to Joanne Fedler, writing mentor and accomplished author, for teaching me the craft and appearing at the perfect time in my life so I could pursue a desire I didn't even know I had when we first crossed paths. And thank you to two women in that group of students, Anna, and Lisa, who have become dear friends and have supported me in ways I will be forever grateful for. Your encouragement and guidance have been like a warm, heartfelt hug. Lisa's time and energy to help edit this book has been invaluable and I can't thank her enough.

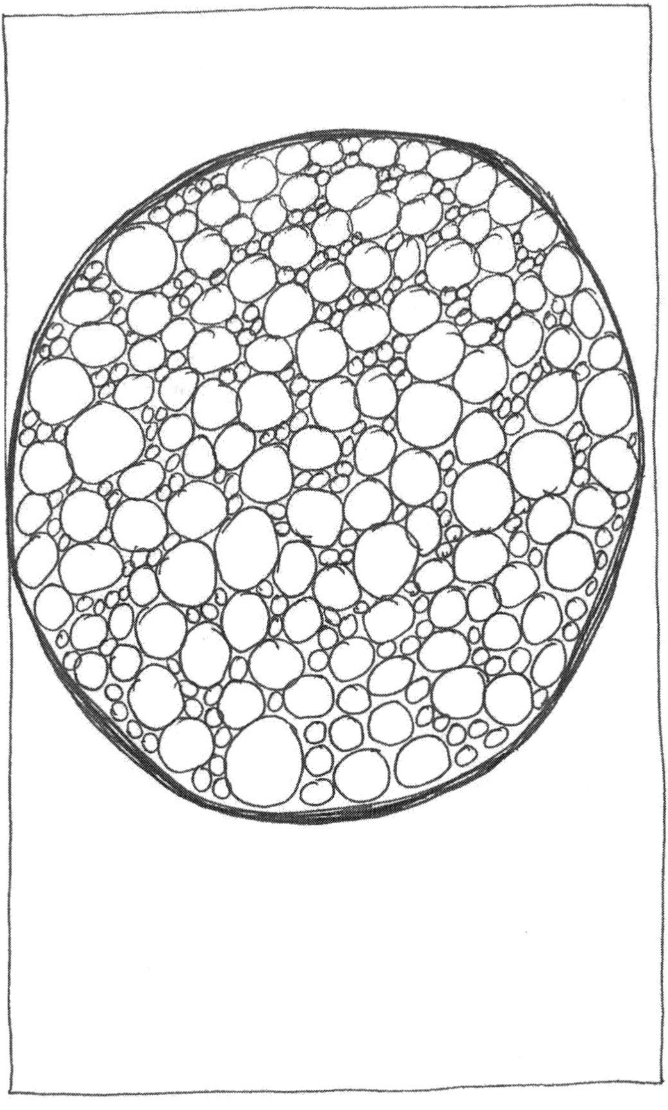

To live a joyful, empowered life of happiness is to stand in your magical, inspired connection to who you really are.

What does it mean to be who you truly are?

It means to give yourself permission to live your most inspired life.

It means you are the creator of your experience. You get to choose what's best for you instead of being a people pleaser and living according to others' judgements and ideals.

It means to connect with your desires and take action for purpose and fulfilment.

It means taking responsibility for everything you feel, then working through it to reconcile the teachings and rise to the growth.

It means to do all these things and invite in opportunities, abundance, and laughter.

It means to follow your own dreams, be aware of how you have become who you are, accept all that is and do the work to change what you need and want to.

It means knowing when to step up and when to soften.

In all of that, is your exquisite experience of humanness.

And glorious, happiness. Oh, so glorious.

Intention: Today, I will ....

Every tear you have cried, every broken bone, and every bruise has been worth it.

You have truly lived.

The heartbreak is the gold that proves you've loved.

The frustrations have led you to great achievements.

The losses have been your sacrifice for success.

What a wise, beautiful soul you are.

Intention: Today, I will ....

Who do you see when you look in the mirror?

When you look past the lines, spots, lumps, and imperfections, see the woman you have become through the richness of your life experiences.

She is brave, strong, and beautiful.

She has a depth of power that is beyond tangible. It is timeless, and emanates ancient wisdom.

She is magical.

She is you.

Intention: Today, I will ....

Be mindful of all the times you say no.

Maybe it's time to say, *"Yes."*

Yes, to experiences, *yes* to opportunities, *yes* to new connections, *yes* to more joy and *yes* to empowerment.

Open up your world of possibilities with one little word.

Yes!

Intention: Today, I will ....

Get out your pom poms and be the cheer squad for those around you.

Their success is your success.

Their wealth is your wealth.

Their love is your love.

Be a genuine, supportive mentor and champion your people.

Intention: Today, I will ....

There's no need to be a *fighter*, or a *warrior*. You also don't need to be *fierce*.

You can just be you, through *ease and grace*.

You can be softer.

You can move slower.

You don't have to keep up with others or heal the way they tell you to.

Do it your way.

Intention: Today, I will ....

Instead of reacting to someone with the need to be right, ask yourself the question, "Does it really matter?"

The compulsion to tell someone they're wrong comes from needing to feel in control.

There's a saying, "Do you want to be right, or happy?"

Intention: Today, I will ....

"I love being older."

Sigourney Weaver

Sometimes, you need to honour the fact that you can't do it and the only answer is to stay in bed.

Give yourself permission to *not* be a martyr.

Intention: Today, I will ....

Pick a day when you will throw out the schedule.

Choose to do whatever you want, without explanation or validation.

Don't tell anyone about it, and don't share it.

Just keep a moment of precious, soul connecting, fulfilment all to yourself.

Be it stillness, be it adventurous, allow it to soak your veins.

Embody your bliss.

Intention: Today, I will ....

Do you struggle to trust people and let them in?

Maybe you expect everyone will let you down, so you build a wall to protect yourself.

It's not your fault. Your experiences have shaped you this way.

If you want to change it, you can.

You start with awareness and noticing how you react to others.

It's safe to let people in. Beautiful connections await.

Intention: Today, I will ....

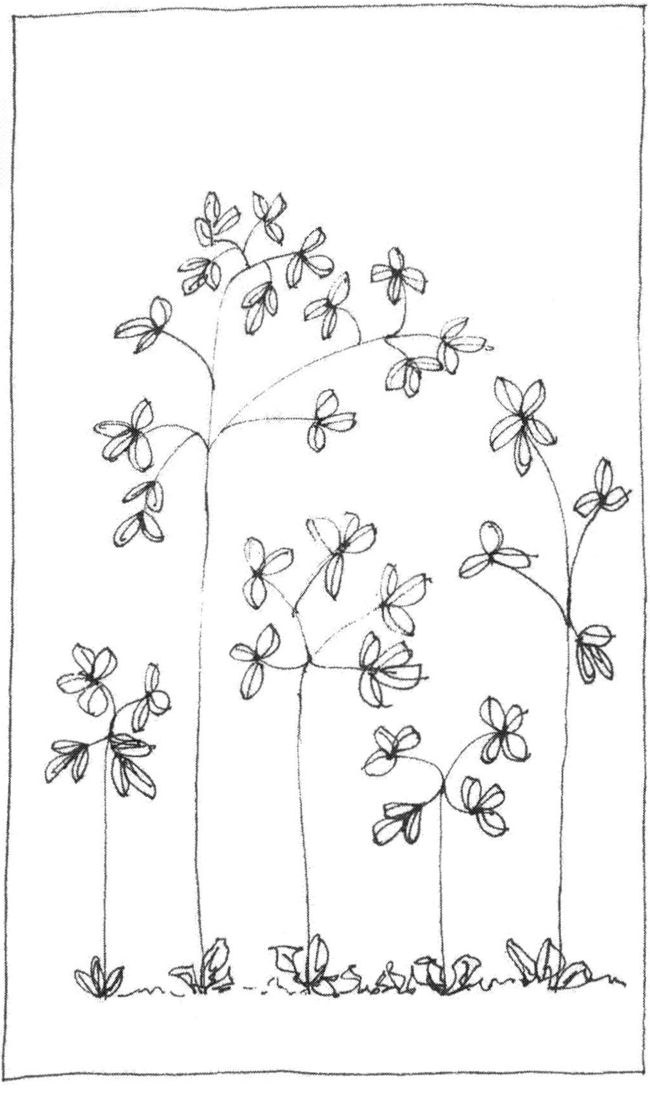

274

You say, *"I could never be like her."*

Damn straight you couldn't, you can only be like you.

"I wish I could be like her."

Oh no you don't, you don't know her story.

"I want to be anyone other than me."

If you were anyone else, the world would weep while grieving for you.

You are perfect. Everyone else knows that too.

Intention: Today, I will ....

Are you great at solving problems and fixing things for others?

Awesome, you're an amazing survivor.

But you may have been in survivor mode for a long time. That's ok, as long as you want to be.

However, if you find too many people come to you for help more often than not, it might be time to set some boundaries.

You may not even be aware this happens. It's a pattern of behaviour established a long time ago.

Notice how often you're asked of your time and energy and consider how you feel about it.
Do you want to change it?

Intention: Today, I will ....

A difficult life doesn't have to continue to feel difficult.

It is more difficult to allow things to stay the same.

Intention: Today, I will ....

Don't care, don't mind, or doesn't matter?

Each is vastly different when considering a situation.

Which will serve you best?

Intention: Today, I will ....

Today is for today.

Tomorrow is for tomorrow.

You can't play tomorrow in today,

And you can't play today in tomorrow.

So let's play, *today*.

Intention: Today, I will ....

Don't place your self-worth in the hands of others.

They will never truly treasure it as it deserves to be held, respected, and honoured.

Don't wait for others to validate your beliefs, dreams, or disappointments.

Each time you look externally for someone to confirm your perspective, just remind yourself it has nothing to do with them, but rather everything to do with you standing in your truth.

Own it.

Intention: Today, I will ....

Some days are just hard.

You're doing great.

Keep going.

You've got this.

Intention: Today, I will ....

"Find ecstasy in life: The mere sense
of living is joy enough."

Emily Dickinson

Regardless of what you do or don't believe about anything in life or death, always believe there are miracles.

They happen for us all the time.

That person who randomly helped you solve your problem? It was a miracle.

That extra money that arrived just in time? A timely miracle.

You waking up today? Boom, miracle!

They may be small sometimes, but they are always powerful.

Intention: Today, I will ....

Life's too short to be normal. Be weird!

Does being different make you less than? Never.

It makes you bold, beautiful, and magnificent.

Some won't like it. Ok, "Bye!"

But others will love you for it. Ok, "Hi!"

Be you and celebrate all that is you.

Don't get to the end of it all wishing you had the courage to be true to yourself. The time is now.

Intention: Today, I will ....

You are *not* many of the things you think you are.

And you *are* many things you think you aren't.

Intention: Today, I will ....

People can't hurt you, they can only touch the parts of you already hurting.

Someone else's behaviour will trigger different meanings within your own psyche that is connected to your own experiences.

No one can *make* you feel anything. You always react according to your own beliefs, thoughts, and feelings.

You are no-one's puppet, and you always get to choose how you respond.

Take back your power.

Choose what's best for your higher good in any given moment.

Intention: Today, I will ....

How powerful would it be if you considered that every single person you meet today could be experiencing their most difficult days, so you treat them with all the kindness, compassion and love you can?

Regardless of who you are, what you do and how you roll, give love first, always, in every situation.

Love changes lives.

Intention: Today, I will ....

Why do people smile at you when they walk past?

Because they are drawn to you when your eyes shine through the vibration of love.

Why do others judge you and make snide remarks as they walk past you?

Because they are drawn to your vibration of love, they are not able to match.

You either mirror people's love for themselves, or what they are not able to feel.

In that moment you gift them the opportunity to learn about themselves. It is then up to them how they respond.

Intention: Today, I will ....

Appreciating all that surrounds you right now brings you joy.

Start with the simple things.

Maybe you haven't noticed them before.

Coffee and sunshine? Or maybe vegemite on toast is your thing.

Go nuts and add some cheese.

Mmm, so much happiness in one little bite!

Intention: Today, I will ....

All those people who told you you're less than perfect?

They were wrong.

Very, very, wrong.

Say it out loud. "I am enough."

Intention: Today, I will ....

The secret to a life of happiness?

One, teeny tiny simple tip.

The *only* thing you're ever required to do,

is...

... give yourself permission to reconnect with joy.

Intention: Today, I will ....

Everything you have done up till now has got you to the now.

Do you want things to remain the same, or do you want things to be different?

Give it some thought, beautiful.

Intention: Today, I will ....

"When you are brave in giving yourself permission
to let go of all you're trying so hard to hold onto,
you will allow happiness to flow through you."

Ali Williams

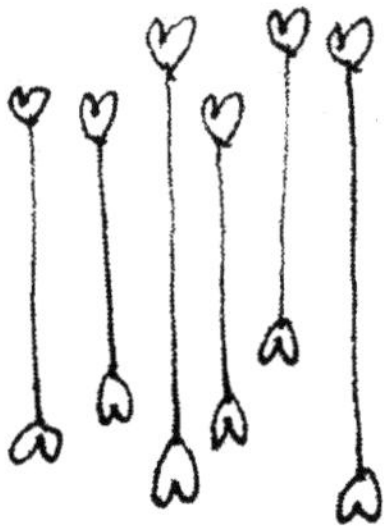

Too often we are way too critical of ourselves.

That self-talk creeps in and you know it's damaging, but it's there and has unpacked its bags.

It may seem too challenging to change.

But you can learn to change things up and soothe that overactive mind.

Your stories aren't true.

You can let them go and send the bags with them.

Imagine, just for a moment, how free you would feel without them.

The results will be glorious.

Intention: Today, I will ....

Life is sometimes like coffee.

How do you take yours, skinny cap maybe, or an almond latte?

Maybe sometimes the cafe gets your order wrong, or it's bitter and too strong.

You can either whinge, or you can calmly ask for another.

If you receive the perfect cup, do you take a moment to breathe in that sweet, robust, velvety goodness as it excites your senses and warms your belly?

Make it as sweet as you like, but pause before each sip.

Inhale deeply.

Don't skull. Take your time.

Intention: Today, I will ....

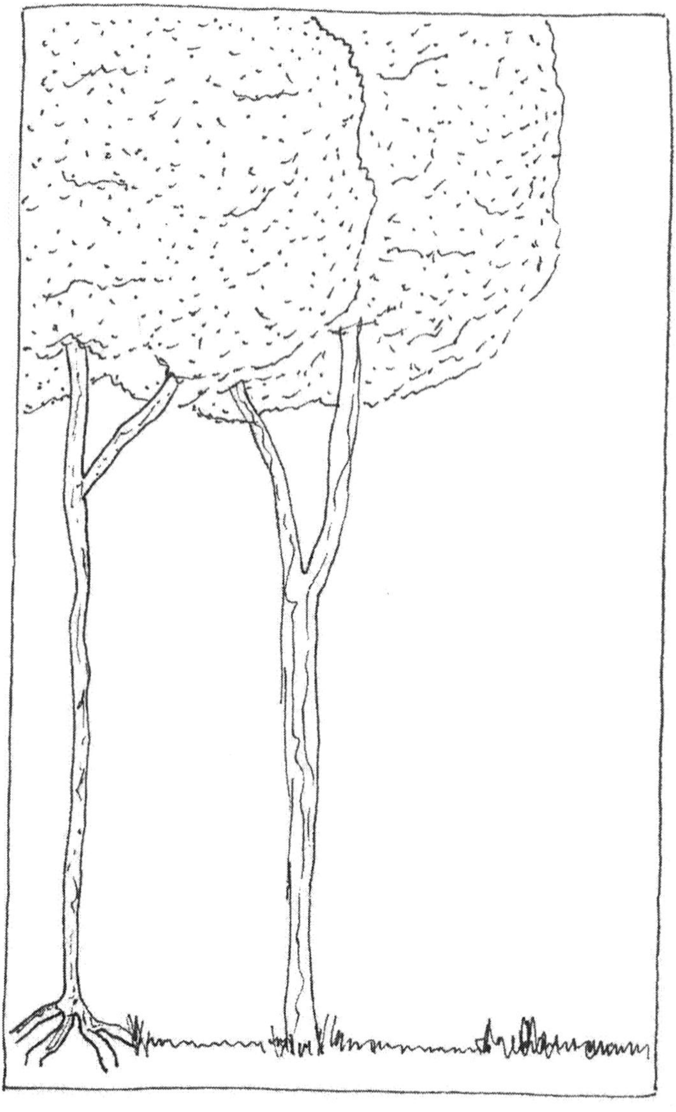

Our programming starts from birth.

How we are nurtured as an infant teaches us about trust.

Between the ages of approximately eighteen months to four years old we then receive our programming around shame, doubt, and guilt.

Were you ever yelled at for not sharing your toys, or told you were a 'naughty girl'? When told over and over we are doing things 'wrong' those negative feelings are created in our brain.

Consider how many times it has been reinforced by others you aren't good enough?

You won't remember many of those times, but your brain will store it in your subconscious with the rest of your collections of thoughts in your memory and meaning library. You don't always go to read those books, but they still sit there on the shelf, gathering dust and they won't move until you read them and soak in the knowledge they offer.

Ditch your shame, doubt, and guilt, they are holding you back.

Intention: Today, I will ....

If everything we did was the safe and logical option we would end up flat lining.

That's ok for some who are happy in that space, but they could be missing out.

The greatest achievers didn't feel safe when they made their life changing decisions ultimately leading to success.

There comes a time when you need to stop questioning and overanalysing, and instead *trust*.

Trust that your burning desire is worth it.

Trust that lying awake in the middle of the night, downloading inspiration, is guidance.

Trust that you will never fail, but grow.

And, trust that you are powerful enough to handle whatever follows.

Intention: Today, I will ....

Get a little wild.

Step outside the square once in a while, if not always.

Just for a moment forget everything you have to do and be for everyone else and take the time to go without shoes.

Leave your perfectly styled hair untamed for the day.

I see you there with your handbag in one hand and coffee in the other. Put them both down and stop for a moment to daydream.

So what if you're a few minutes late.

Don't worry if you're not there to solve everyone's problems. Not your responsibility, by the way.

Go through your day so that when you get to the end of it you say, "Daaammmnnn girl, you did good today and it's a great day to be alive!"

Intention: Today, I will . . . .

Are you one of those people who says, "I don't have a creative bone in my body?"

Yes, you do.

When talking about creativity it is important to remember 'Big C' and 'Little C'.

Each time you solve a problem, answer a question, create a meal, organise a family function, plant out your garden, create a spreadsheet and coordinate an outfit you are tapping into your 'Little C'.

Some of us can connect with our 'Big C' through grand gestures like what we see in artists, writers, architects, builders and so on.

Even though you may not think you are creative, you have the potential for Big C as much as anyone. Just let go of the comparison to the Picasso's of this world.

Using your creativity lights up the parts of your brain that calm your nervous system, regulate emotions, help with problem solving and enhance your happiness.

So, get creating, whatever that looks like for you.

Intention: Today, I will ....

Get grounded and touch the grass.

Put your phone down and lay there for a long time while you watch the sky.

Stand a little longer in the shower as you feel the nourishing warmth on your skin.

Dance like it's Saturday night.

There is far more fun to be had when you make it all about you momentarily, even just for one day.

Intention: Today, I will ....

Your back has been up against a wall many times and yet you thrive in your resilience as you carry on through all that is necessary and obligatory.

You are totally amazing.

Intention: Today, I will ....

Often, we spend too much time and energy thinking about how we are going to do something or make something happen.

The secret is to stop doing so much.

Stop pushing.

Stop stressing.

Stop sacrificing.

To achieve more, do less.

Stop trying so hard, and instead slow down and allow your inspiration to flow.

Intention: Today, I will . . . .

It's no good to pay lip service to your favourite affirmation such as, "I'm going to make a million bucks this year," and then be an arsehole in every other area of your life.

You have to live and breathe it.

Embody your everyday thoughts of joy, passion, knowing and belief.

Breathe them in, let them bathe your blood.

Your everyday thoughts will become your everyday experience, whichever you choose to focus on.

Are you complaining? Stop.

Are you a victim? Choose to let go of blame.

Hanging on to devastating trauma or adversity? Find the right person to help you move through it.

Wondering why things haven't turned out how you've wanted?

Start with you. Every, single, time. Then everything will change.

Intention: Today, I will ....

There are some people in this humanness of our existence who feel so insecure about themselves that seeing you fail makes them feel better about themselves.

Your success is a reminder of what they don't have, or what they haven't done.

Don't apologise, nor justify your achievements. You are not responsible for how they feel.

If they acknowledge the lesson, they are ready to expand.

Keep doing you. You've invested in yourself, and your success and happiness are inspiring.
Keep showing up, you are worthy of enjoying all the good things in life.

Intention: Today, I will ....

"Life shrinks or expands in proportion to one's courage."

Anaïs Nin

Are you aware of people's behaviour?

Recognising the supportive stayers from the energy vampires will enable the superficial to be revealed as you become more aware.

Choose carefully who you trust. Only some will want to encourage and support you unconditionally.

Anyone else who isn't there for the same love and respect that you give may only cause disappointment.

Consider the people around you who value you, and themselves.

This will be a nurturing exchange.

Intention: Today, I will ....

Have you ever considered there may be another possibility of how you may see things?

You perceive a situation or individual a certain way but are you making assumptions based on what you *think* you see?

Look deeper.

Maybe the key to resolving a situation is not shackled in your way but is instead ready to be released through an alternative perspective.

Intention: Today, I will ....

Be open to noticing small miracles.

Those moments that make you smile when you notice the message, the image, the word, or the feeling that came out of nowhere.

Embrace the synchronicities.

Your heart will flutter, and your eyes will close, just for a second, as you smile with the knowing of the meaning.

There are no coincidences, only magic.

Intention: Today, I will ....

Season, reason, lifetime.

Think of all the people in your life and how they have fit into each timespan.

Some have been part of your life for a fleeting moment but made an impact.

Some came into your life for a while and then drifted.

And then there's those who are your soul family. Strong connections that expand across all space and time, based on mutual respect, acceptance, and love.

Some of those people in the past have hurt you, and some have left deep wounds. But in every relationship, no matter what the reason for it ending, there is always a gift of insight.

These people have been your teachers, and it is up to you to discover what lessons of empowerment you learned in each circumstance.

Every, single, one of them.

Intention: Today, I will ....

Everything we have been taught in the past has been designed to suppress, oppress, and detest.

"Don't cry," it's weak. "Don't get angry," it's toxic. "Suck it up and get on with it."
We've got to the point of never allowing ourselves to be vulnerable because we have been shut down too many times.

Inner tension builds without a release.

Instead, give yourself permission to feel all the feels, without judgement.

Crying is innate. Healthy anger is innate. Fear is also innate and protects us from potential dangers but looking past it will bring relief.

It is in the letting go that healing is embraced.
It's time to protest past restraints and find freedom in self-expression.

Intention: Today, I will ....

How often have you felt disappointed when things didn't turn out as planned?

We tend not to dwell on little things such as missing a green light on the way to work that makes us late, but the big things in life such as difficult relationships and unfulfilling jobs can be much harder to move on from.

Consider, though, the longer and tighter you hold on, the more you will suffer.

Accept that all is not as you had hoped and do something to change it, or make peace with deciding not to.

Making a decision either way will help you release anxious energy.

Intention: Today, I will ....

We don't always understand the significance of loss in our lives.

Why must we suffer such grief?

It runs deep, and leaves holes in our soul that may never be filled.

It is in our healing that we connect with the inner knowing of a bigger purpose.

There is always opportunity for growth and transformation in our greatest losses.

Trust that you will find your own peace and understanding.

You will heal, and you will make sense of it all.

Intention: Today, I will ....

Allowing yourself to forgive is freedom.

Holding onto resentment will hurt you.

It can destroy relationships and steal time you may never get back.

Forgive yourself first, then forgive others.

It's not in your best interests to be holding on to that pain.

Who, or what, do you need to forgive today?

You will feel lighter for it.

Intention: Today, I will ....

Strong women don't always make a lot of noise.

Some of them quietly step out from the depths of all that held them back to rise up and claim their space in the world.

They carve their own path without the need to shout from the roof tops as the rest watch on and admire from afar, wishing they were the same.

These women often prefer not to be placed on a pedestal but instead quietly immerse in a graceful dance through the next chapter of life.

Never underestimate those women, there is much to learn from them, and if you are one of them, you have much to teach others.

Intention: Today, I will ....

As for the experiment, over time it showed that those children who waited were more successful at school, had lower rates of substance abuse and had better health outcomes.

Would you eat the single marshmallow, or would you allow yourself to wait for the greater gain?

Intention: Today, I will ....

We live in an instant society. We can pretty much get anything we want with a click of our fingers.

While this is convenient, it's also messing with our ability to feel genuinely happy.

In the 1960s a famous study called the 'Marshmallow Experiment' was conducted on children aged around four years old.

They were given one marshmallow and told that they could eat it in that moment, or they could wait, after which time they would be rewarded with a whole plate of marshmallows.

This study focused on instant gratification versus delayed gratification.

Instant gratification engages dopamine in our brains which gives us that rush of joy when we receive something as a reward. However, it can pass quickly, and we may end up feeling regret.

On the other hand, delayed gratification stimulates serotonin which is our happy hormone.

Think impulsive decisions versus carefully considered decisions. There is more often greater happiness associated with the latter.

"Joy is what happens to us when we allow ourselves
to recognise how good things really are."

Marianne Williamson

Some days require extra levels of self-compassion.

Give yourself credit for all you are doing.

You've got this.

Maybe you didn't do something perfectly.

Maybe you lost your shit a few times recently.

And, maybe you had no idea how to do something.

That's ok, you can take one step at a time.

Grab a pen and paper and write a list of all the great things you're accomplishing.

Focus on that and give yourself a high five.

Intention: Today, I will ....

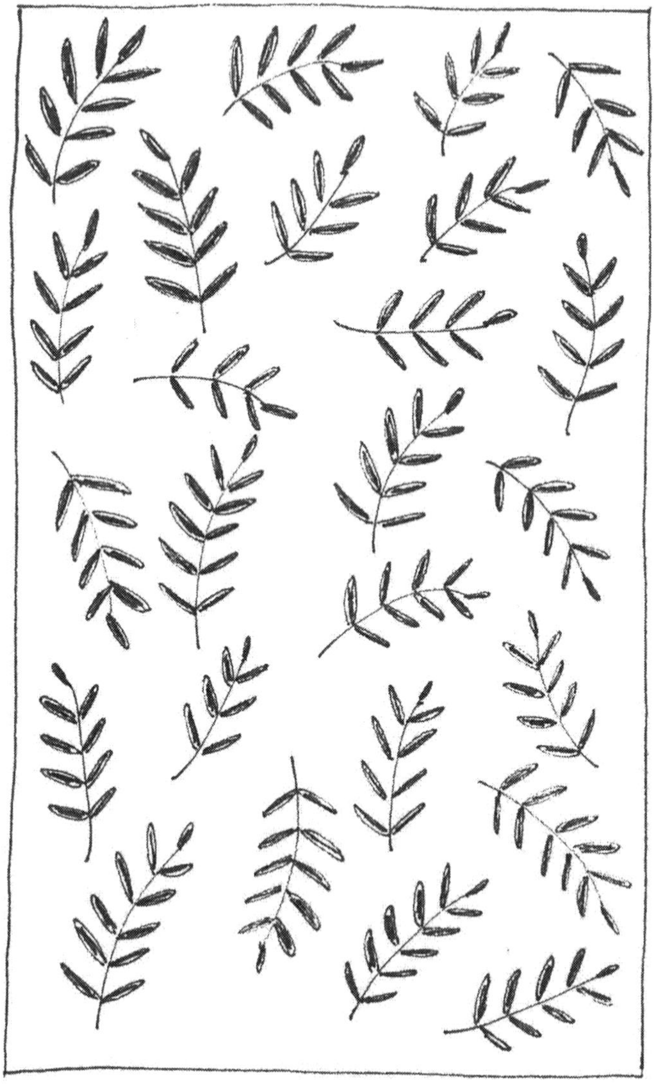

A woman who is unapologetic about her authenticity is enigmatic.

She moves differently. She smiles with her eyes and commands a presence that others notice when she walks into a room.

She knows not everyone will understand her, and accepts that.

She knows each decision she makes will be for her higher good.

She also knows it's important to prioritise her own wellbeing to be at her best for those who need her most.

She is her most beautiful, when embracing her true nature.

Intention: Today, I will ....

You can take the predictable path through life and follow everyone else, or you can mix things up, get uncomfortable, take risks, feel scared as hell, and thrive.

Is it always going to pay off? Well yes, one way or the other.

A powerful quote (author unknown) is, "You can never lose, you can only ever win or learn."

Even if something doesn't work out, it's just a dog leg turn in the right direction.

Get brave, take risks, and get uncomfortable.

You never know where it might lead you.

Intention: Today, I will ....

There is nothing more blissful than resting in silence.

For many people this can be a very difficult thing to do. But when you do, it is healing.

With practice, the noise will quieten, the inspiration will flow, and you will come to crave this sacred space.

Intention: Today, I will ....

Taking the easier road through life and fitting into a one-size-fits-all box might seem enticing.

It is initially less draining to do what everyone expects of you, suck it up and be at peace with it all.

But in truth, this may only make things harder in the long run.

When you have the feeling that you want to do things differently resistance may present itself.

Until we are ready to own it, life can get tricky.

When you start to wrestle with the lid of the box you feel exhausted, relationships may get rocky and work or business doesn't seem to flow any more.

This is your opportunity to take responsibility and become who you are meant to be.

You're more a bespoke kind of woman. Right?

Intention: Today, I will ....

This thing called life is no smooth gentle drive around the block.

It's a bit more like a four-wheeled trek over the rockiest, steepest mountain with a sheer drop on the other side. You may even lose a wheel and break your axle!

You packed the car with the anticipation of enjoying the day out, only to be faced with disaster. Then in the midst of all the chaos, without really knowing how things will turn out, you found a way through your challenges and ended up laughing about the events of the day and reflecting on what you will do differently next time.

We all have good intentions, and sometimes things go wrong.

Whatever happens, we can be sure to follow up one adventure with another.

Pack your picnic hamper, campers, and strap yourself in.

Embrace the ride.

Intention: Today, I will ....

The only thing guaranteed in life is that nothing stays the same.

It's easy to get caught up in our energy being consumed with issues that won't exist in another day, week or month.

Through accepting change and adapting, life gets easier.

The more set in our ways we are, the more resistant to change we will be.

Resistance creates disharmony.

Let go, embrace change and go with it.

Oh, how the mind boggles at the potential for unexpected possibilities.

Intention: Today, I will ....

When you consider how much time you spend criticising and doubting yourself, are those thoughts taking up too much real estate in your heart and mind?

What if you could change the game just by asking them to move out and invite in self-love and self-belief instead?

Intention: Today, I will ....

Your own healing changes lives.

Not just your own, but those who came before you and those who will follow.

Family wounds can be passed through generations and it is up to us to disrupt these patterns so they stop, here and now.

When you see the younger generation repeating destructive behaviours of their parents, it will continue, if not changed.

When we see them break away from old family patterns to do things differently, they are healing old patterns and ending the cycle.

You don't have to do things the same as has always been done before.

You can heal, and in doing so, change the future in creating healing for others.

Intention: Today, I will ....

Hold yourself in a space of self-compassion when you feel vulnerable.

Allow all your emotions to flow.

It may be messy, beautiful, complicated, and fragile.

Honour everything you feel on the not so perfect days.

Intention: Today, I will ....

"The more you take responsibility for
your past and present, the more you are
able to create the future you seek."

Unknown

Sometimes you just have to throw your arms in the air, laugh, and say, "I won't do that again!"

Our biggest mistakes are profound moments in our lives.

Self-acceptance is always the key to moving forward.

Laughing boosts your immune system and happy hormones and also helps to regulate emotions.

Laughing at yourself also helps to observe the issue rather than internalise it.

Laugh more often at yourself and allow self-forgiveness.

No one ever gets a perfect path but there's gold in the moments that go pear-shaped.

Intention: Today, I will ....

At some point in life, most of us will have been drawn into the toxicity of a bitter person who tells untruths about us.

It can leave you feeling helpless and powerless. It stings.

Don't waste your energy trying to put spot fires out.

Those who cannot see clearly may need to be left behind.

Share your time and love with those who see the truth for what it is.

Everyone else will make a choice that is best for them.

It has little to do with you.

Whatever happens, you will be ok.

Intention: Today, I will ....

Avoidant behaviours are counterintuitive.

Avoiding the tough conversations negatively reinforces the angst around the issues that need to be discussed.

Avoiding taking responsibility for your actions perpetuates drama.

Avoiding doing the work on yourself, leads to a life of suffering.

It might be uncomfortable initially when stepping up and approaching life's difficult situations head on.

On the other side, however, is your freedom.

Intention: Today, I will ....

Let go of how you expected things to turn out.

Let go of everything that didn't work.

Keep your eyes open for those little kicks in the butt. Seek to understand how the outcome might not be what you want but are instead what you need.

Go with it, it might be pleasantly surprising.

Intention: Today, I will ....

We all speak our own language of love.

What fills your cup will be different for others.

It takes a special connection with another to appreciate moments together while holding space for each other's interpretations.

Seek to understand how you express the language of love and be open to considering the same for others and how you can enjoy communication on a new level.

Intention: Today, I will ....

Sometimes the biggest blessings can be disguised as the most challenging adversities.

Even when something feels confronting, there is always an opportunity to surrender, go with it and wait for the pivotal moment you will be grateful for.

It will come. It's inevitable. It just depends how you look at it.

Intention: Today, I will ....

Protect your time and energy.

Don't allow them to become everyone else's commodity. Be choosy where, when, and with whom you share them.

Intention: Today, I will . . . .

Whatever you choose to do today is feeding your mind.

What feeds your mind creates your thoughts and feelings. Whatever you think and feel will determine your actions.

Your actions create your experiences and opportunities.

Your experiences and opportunities then feed your mind.

You are building the circle.

Choose carefully what you include in it.

Intention: Today, I will ....

Your words are powerful.

They can be as beautiful and encouraging as much as they can be destructive.

They hold great responsibility.

At its finest, your language filters out into the world as a love filled miracle that caresses and dances around others' hearts.

At its worst it can fuel the momentum of hostility and tear down the very fibre of one's being with one fiery unchecked exclamation.

Savour your words before you spit them out.

When your verbal utterances taste sweet, they have a way of finding their way back to you with extra sugar 'n spice, and all things nice.

Intention: Today, I will ....

You know that girl. When entering a room, she makes her presence known and appears to be the most confident person in the middle of the crowd.

She might be outgoing in public, but behind closed doors she criticises herself and loathes herself.

She doesn't let people in. It is her survival.

She doesn't know how to love herself. She will only learn how when she embraces her vulnerability.

Leave behind your assumptions of her. Instead, understand there may be suffering behind the façade.

Intention: Today, I will ....

When your partner says something that triggers you, is it their fault?

No.

It's your programming and life experiences that have created that meaning.

You can choose to enter the storm and fuel negative momentum, or, you can choose to take responsibility and remember your reactions are up to you.

Ever heard the saying, "He who angers you, controls you?"

Walk away, and take a breather.

Talk about it after you have processed the emotion.

By no means allow yourself to be walked on, nor should you walk upon, but instead turn it around into a moment of reconciliation.

Intention: Today, I will ....

"A smile is the best makeup a girl could wear."

Marilyn Monroe

When you know, you know.

When you have that feeling you are on your way to a bigger purpose, trust that it will all fall into place when it's meant to.

Don't get caught up in the how's, who's, and when's.

Only ever take action that is for your higher good, and understand that there is a certain element you don't get to control.

Everything will fall into place when you can let go and roll with it.

Intention: Today, I will ....

As she pauses with a gaze into the mirror she says, "I'm done with feeling less than. Today I will do things differently."

And therein lies, in that one little decision, her power to change her world.

Intention: Today, I will ....

Rest, beautiful woman.

Your soul creates magic through nourishment and stillness.

What do you need today?

Listen to your body and what it is asking you for.

Your peace is more precious than any load of washing or grocery shop.

Intention: Today, I will ....

If you are surrounded by people who only want to tear you down to feel better about themselves, it's time to move on.

Be mindful who you trust.

If they lift you up, they are worthy of your time and energy.

If they aren't with you in the ordinary, they don't belong in your extraordinary.

What you bring to the table is powerful.

Only set a place for those who celebrate you.

Intention: Today, I will ....

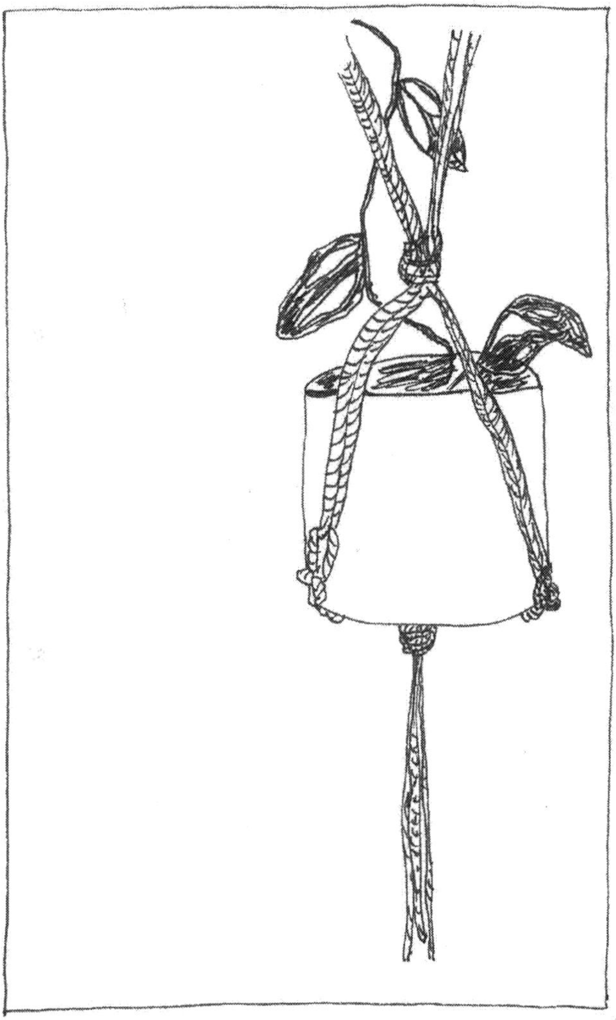

Free your spirit from the heaviness of obligation in all the boxes that you've tried to fit in.

Create your own.

Intention: Today, I will ....

You know the old saying, "If you want something done, do it yourself?"

We have all said it, usually after waiting on or relying on someone else. Our patience runs out, or a deadline looms, and we end up take action.

Are you fed up with waiting for someone else to fix things or give you the answers?

They won't, and if you expect them to you are sabotaging your own peace of mind.

Be mindful of expectation, it is a sneaky manipulator. The greater it is, the greater the potential for disappointment.

Intention: Today, I will ....

Do you try to shove your emotions into a bottle and stop them with a cork?

If you continue to suppress them, they will eventually need to go somewhere.

You can't ignore them for long.

You know the feeling of laughing so hard your stomach and cheeks hurt? Imagine trying to hold that in. It would be near impossible. All that energy would build to the point of explosion!

Your emotions are your guidance system. If you're unwell or in pain, your physical body is communicating that it needs you to do the work to release the negative energy.

Holding all that pain, guilt, and sadness within can only mean one thing.

You are choosing to suffer.

And suffer, you will.

Find safe ways to process your emotions. Your wellbeing depends on it.

Intention: Today, I will ....

As women, we too often compare ourselves to others and only see what separates us.

This will never allow us to realise our own strengths.

If we acknowledge in others what we wish for ourselves, without judgement, and instead embrace the opportunity to be inspired, we can only grow.

Play big and champion others. Supporting them allows us to also learn from them.

Intention: Today, I will ....

Connect with your bravery and decide that it is time, now, to do the work and create change your life.

You may not think you are ready, but waiting for the *right* time may never come.

You may also think you don't have the energy, time or money.

When you value your wellbeing and happiness, all three will magically become available and the perfect people to support you will appear.

How many times have you wondered how differently you could be living your life but have no idea how to change things?

You start with a decision to put yourself first.

Create moments every day when you honour your transformation and practice non-negotiable positive behaviours.

Everything changes when you give yourself permission to take action for your wellbeing.

Intention: Today, I will ....

"The strongest women I know aren't always the happiest. The happiest women I know are at peace with why they've needed to be strong."

Ali Williams

Each time you smile, you can't help but feel good.

You can choose to frown, or you can choose to lighten up and turn things around.

You can change someone's day in an instant through sharing your pearly whites of positivity!

What if, just for today, you smiled at everyone.

Conduct an experiment, and consider it an act of kindness towards others.

Observe others' behaviour when you smile at them and notice how their energy changes.

Then notice how much your own energy lifts.

A simple happiness gesture that weaves its way through the thread of humanity.

Intention: Today, I will . . . .

You know those days, when you've given everything of yourself to others.

You allow yourself to end up so depleted that it is an effort to function.

Call your energy back. It is precious.

The first thing needed is self-care.

If you don't take care of yourself, who will?

Teach those around you to value their own wellbeing first by showing them you value yourself.

Intention: Today, I will ....

When we hold onto things too tightly that don't serve us, we can only find sadness.

If we cling to dysfunctional relationships, past hurts or lost opportunities we hold ourselves back.

Let go.

It might be the hardest thing you will ever do, but in time you will realise it is a step towards happiness.

Don't be frightened.

You will move forward.

Letting go of the negative anchors in your life will make way for your discovery of new passions and connections.

Intention: Today, I will ....

There is often nothing warm and fuzzy about taking responsibility for creating change at the deepest level of your being.

This is why we avoid it for so long and stumble along in denial.

In the beginning, shining light on what we need to work on may feel scary and unsafe.

Your brain's job is to keep you safe, and any new behaviours you try to incorporate may initially be perceived as a threat.

Your brain will react by firing off warning signals. It will default to its programming to cling to the familiar. Think, "Danger, Will Robinson!"

Acknowledge the discomfort and remind yourself it is temporary.

Your brain will adjust, and you will create new patterns as you weaken old ones.

Hang in there.

Your future self will be worth it. In fact, it will be glorious.

Intention: Today, I will ....

Ever had the sensation of butterflies in your belly without knowing why?

When we live in flow, we invite in opportunities that may not yet be understood.

Just go with it.

Good stuff will happen.

It just will.

Intention: Today, I will ....

Is it a bad day?

Or is it a challenging moment?

If it is a bad day, take some time out. Take a few deep breaths and close your eyes.

List three good things, even the tiniest, like the smell of a fresh cup of coffee. Think about that instead.

If it is a blip, then carry on, you've got this.

Intention: Today, I will ....

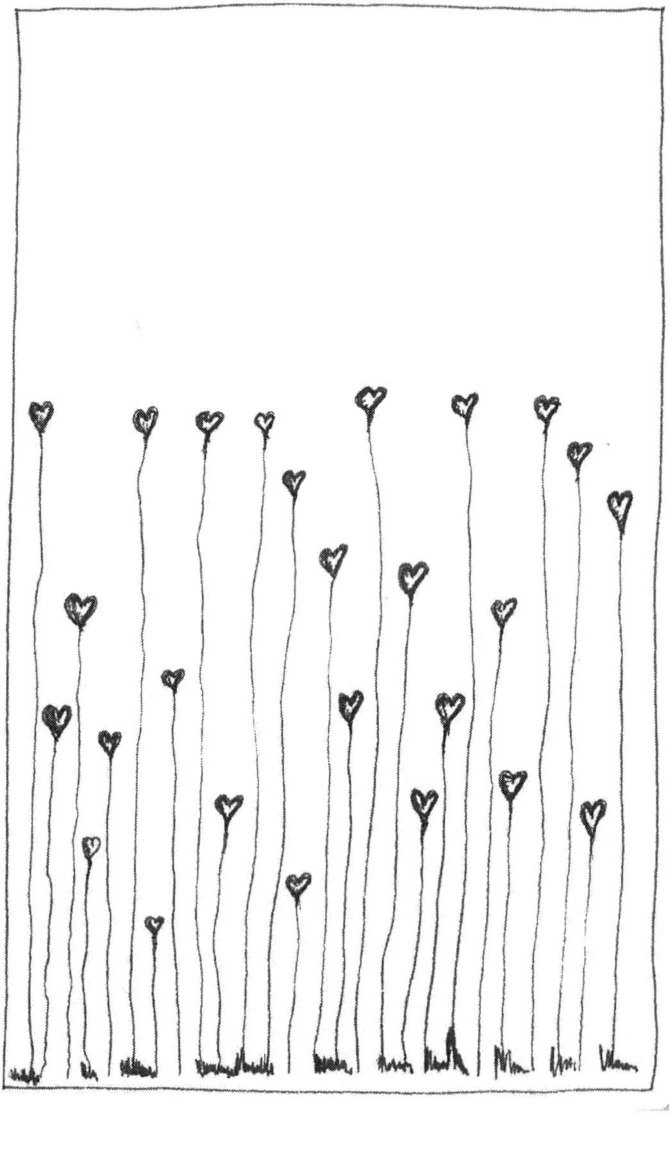

Sound, breath, and movement are all essential restorative practices for our health and wellbeing.

Soft sound through meditation, music, and nature quiet the mind.

Deep, slow breathing restores our nervous system.

Gentle movement increases blood flow while releasing stagnant energy and toxins from our muscles and organs.

Self-nurture is healing.

In healing, is enlightenment.

Intention: Today, I will ....

Your ability to stand up again and again after being knocked to the ground only to become stronger will ignite your innate leadership potential that others seek.

You can be the strength for those who wish they could thrive as you have.

There will be people admiring your resilience from afar.

Use your voice to be their voice.

Wave your placard of inspiration.

Step out and claim your story as the pathway to the front of the crowd.

Intention: Today, I will ....

We all want to belong somewhere; it is the human nature of survival. But we can easily compromise who we are.

We can choose to do the monkey dance of keeping up appearances, or we can choose to be honest with ourselves and live authentically.

Owning who you are is freedom.

Being who you think others want you to be is obligation.

Do you know who you are and what you want?

The world needs you to be you.

Your true belonging is in showing up as yourself.

Intention: Today, I will ....

Never confuse peace with boredom.

Intention: Today, I will ....

"When someone else's happiness is
your happiness, that is love."

Lana Del Rey

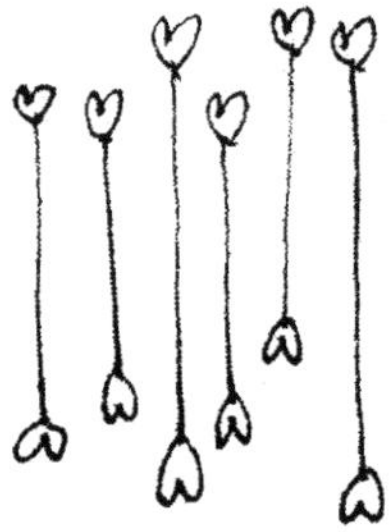

Anxiety is the art of worrying about something that hasn't happened yet.

It pulls you back from being truly present and embracing the here and now.

We can unknowingly amplify the discomfort by trying to avoid those things creating the angst.

If you don't like being in crowds, the more you avoid being in that situation the more you reinforce your anxiety.

It is a cycle that you have the power to interrupt, if you choose to train your brain to think differently.

It is possible.

You start with awareness.

Believe you can create the change you long for.

Intention: Today, I will ....

Stop saying life is hard.

Stop saying life is short.

What do you want it to be? Beautiful, joyful and successful?

Say that.

Intention: Today, I will ....

Everything in your life is connected to self-love.

It is the deep thread that creates loving, lasting relationships.

It is your energy of love that attracts success and opportunity.

It is the potent soul medicine for your healing.

It is your freedom from judgement, expectation, and disappointment.

It is more than life. It is living.

Your self-love will guide you forward in every single circumstance.

Your self-love is your empowerment.

Intention: Today, I will ....

Give yourself permission to do things differently.

Move on from relying on other people to give their approval.

Let go of your expectations of others.

Be less afraid of judgement.

Avoid making assumptions to justify your own need for answers.

Make different decisions.

Intention: Today, I will ....

If you could do anything in your wildest imagination and inspiration, what would it be?

If there were no limitations, no excuses, and no doubts, where would you be?

And if someone knocked on your door, held you hand and said, "Let's go do it," would you?

Just think about that for a minute.

If your answer was no, maybe you are your own limitation.

If your answer was yes, then you don't need to wait for anyone to hold your hand.

Intention: Today, I will ....

Sometimes, we don't always see the war that is erupting within our loved ones until we are caught up in it.

We can find ourselves on the receiving end of the complicated labyrinth of their own suffering, loathing and dissatisfaction.

We can see their beauty and know their potential, but can also see the devastation of their self-destruction.

We do all we can to help and support them but we can never create change in their lives. They must choose to do the work.

We can only choose acceptance, to avoid suffering for yourself.

Surrender to the knowing that you cannot fix anyone, and you cannot force them to heal, your way.

You can endlessly support them and ensure their safety, but they must find their own way through their storm.

Intention: Today, I will ....

There is something so painful about remaining silent for fear of reprisal.

You feel it brewing, that thing you want to say, but you are afraid.

Afraid of judgement and consequences. Afraid of the path that may be forever paved, without a way to go back.

We sometimes hold onto our words so fiercely that they settle into our body until they rage.

Allow the release.

Know your worth and speak your truth but first decide if it is for your benefit.

If you cannot set free your words, find a way to let go of the heaviness.

You have enough to carry without the burden of your forbidden honesty.

Intention: Today, I will ....

Striving to be perfect is old school.

Authenticity is where the wise wander.

Letting go of the need to be perfect is the sweetest taste of freedom.

The gift of ageing graces us with this knowing.

If only the younger generation understood how exhausting it is.

Intention: Today, I will ....

Do you successfully set boundaries? Maybe you need to and you don't know it yet.

Consider the people in your life who demand your time and attention, but don't ever give anything in return.

It is admirable to help someone else but it is holding you back when it becomes consuming.

We live in an instant society, and most people expect a response to their needs straight away.

Teenagers demand an immediate reply to their text message, clients expect an immediate answer to their email and there are those friends who want you to drop everything to help them.

Establishing boundaries can get uncomfortable before it gets better, but they are essential for your wellbeing.

Be ok with putting your own needs first. If someone else's needs are not life and death, prioritise your availability when it works for you.

Or, you can even say no. The world will not end if you do, unless you're Superwoman, then we may need you to act quickly!

Give yourself permission to set boundaries.

Intention: Today, I will ....

Beautiful people do not just happen.

They make a decision.

They choose to learn, grow, live in truth and ditch judgement.

They are often inspired to embrace consciousness through self-modelling from others, or they rise up after adversity.

Regardless of our experiences, we always have the choice to bathe in all that is beautiful in our own eyes.

To see the beautiful, is to be beautiful.

Intention: Today, I will ....

"Stop shrinking to fit places you've outgrown."

Furaha Joyce

She who braves and embraces the magic of darkness will step forward to the front of the line and raise their hand with willingness, as the universe delivers her rewards.

How far have you already leaped through the layers of growth on offer?

Embrace your experiences.

They are presented to you, because you are ready.

Intention: Today, I will ....

Your joy in seeing someone else embrace their success and happiness, comes from a place of self-love.

Resentment in believing you deserve their success instead, rages from a place of envy and rejection.

Know that we are all deserving of success and happiness.

We sometimes want what someone else has because we feel a sense of lack.

The truth is that no one can expect external *things* to bring happiness without experiencing disappointment and disillusion at some point.

Your happiness rests in seeing the joy right now, even if it is for someone else.

Intention: Today, I will ....

If you open your eyes to see all that you haven't before, your world will become all that you hadn't expected.

Often we are consumed by all we need to do while running on autopilot.

We miss opportunities to see beauty in little things.

Simple moments of mindfulness will allow so much more into your existence.

What you see activates your brain into creating memories and meaning.

If you see ugly, you will continue to see ugly.

But if you see all worth seeing, you will feel all that is worth embracing.

Intention: Today, I will ....

When we go through a rupture in our lives, it feels like we are in pieces.

Those moments don't make sense at the time. The heaviness in your core may not be visible, but it is nauseating.

Then one day you start to put those pieces back together, although they settle in a little differently.

You may not feel the same, and you may look different to others.

When the last piece is added, it is a sweet satisfaction of completion.

There is so much good in never being the same again.

Intention: Today, I will ....

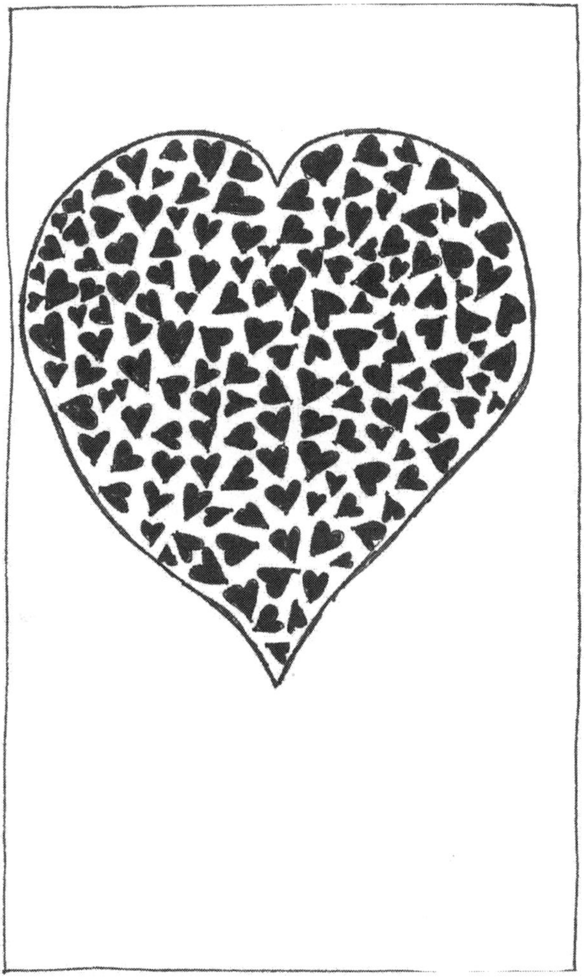

Trying to fit both worry and faith into your everyday thinking can be exhausting.

Your brain can only focus on one thing at a time.

Directing your energy into worrying only perpetuates more of the same and distracts you from finding practical solutions for your problems.

Focusing your energy on faith is a force so powerful it can create change in incredible ways.

Remember what you are capable of achieving.

Intention: Today, I will ....

What are the things you love doing that make you feel alive?

The things that make you want to skip a little when you walk because you can't wait.

The things that fill your heart so much it could almost burst. When you can't breathe properly, because even for just a brief moment you are so happy that you are transported into another realm.

The things that make you want to smile, sing and dance.

Do those things, and do them often.

Intention: Today, I will ....

Get connected to your inner knowing.

It will guide you, every time.

You will know where to go, who to be with and what to do.

You will also know when to leave, when to stand firm and when to say, "No."

You won't need to be right. You will know it's not about you, and you will know what doesn't serve you.

You will know when to get loud, and you will know when to smile through your silence.

You will also know when and where to share your sparkly cosmic intuitive awesomeness.

Intention: Today, I will ....

As you awoke today after sleeping away all that was yesterday, your body has regenerated and healed.

Your soul has awakened after surrendering to deep rest and renewal.

The world lays down at your feet as the goddess in you stands up to claim your first steps into the day.

Today is for you.

Embrace all that is gifted in the new morning.

Intention: Today, I will ....

Are there people around you who are reactive towards you?

Here's the truth of the matter;

What they don't like in you, is showing them something they need to acknowledge within themselves.

If they are aware and invested in their own growth, they will recognise the opportunity to learn more about themselves.

If they are the victim, they will direct their blame to ease their angst.

You are their teacher in that moment.

See the opportunity in the discomfort, and have compassion. For them, and yourself.

Intention: Today, I will ....

"We're expected to feel happiness only with grand gestures or big things that are comparable to other people's experiences – but joy is a state of everything being enough."

Devi Brown

When you continue to try and nurture relationships with people who don't have your back, we continue to bruise.

When we impose our own expectations onto others it becomes a tug of war with disappointment and abandonment for ourselves.

Set yourself free.

Set them free.

Your most connected people who love you will lift you up, energise you and cheer you on. They also love themselves and willingly give love without obligation.

Reserve your love for those who understand how precious it is.

Intention: Today, I will ....

How present are you right now?

Today gives you the opportunity to be mindful that life is happening in this very minute.

Not yesterday.

Not tomorrow.

Now.

Did you know that you can slow down time when you embrace the beauty of a simplistic moment?

It's epic time bending stuff.

Intention: Today, I will ....

Some days we do life like a goddess, and some days are a messy.

When we expand it can get bumpy, then it gets beautiful, then bumpy, then beautiful again.

That. Is. Life.

We learn. We grow.

Accepting all that is in the good, bad, and ugly allows your transformation into graceful and gutsy.

Wherever you are today, somewhere between goddess and fragile, you are still incredibly beautiful.

Intention: Today, I will ....

Making decisions about what to do next can be overwhelming. Especially in the midst of change.

How do we know if we are making the right choices?

We are so afraid of making the wrong ones that we search for confirmation and meaning to guide us. We look everywhere and anywhere for the answers, except within.

If you stop, be still, and listen, your heart will whisper to you.

It will always show you the way.

Intention: Today, I will ....

We spend too much of our time compromising our own enjoyment in life.

Eating that particular food will cause us to feel regret these days, but in the past it was enjoyable and the reward centre in our brain connected the experience to wanting more.

You know you don't want to attend that party because you don't feel up to it, but in the past your memory associated saying 'no' with the meaning of guilt and shame.

You want to simplify your material existence, but somewhere in the past you were programmed to believe that having less means you are less.

You buy that dress, wear it once and then it sits in your wardrobe because in the past you socially observed that buying new things was somehow fulfilling.

Change it up.

Consider your decisions, and do that spark-joy thing!

Intention: Today, I will ....

Regardless of the arse kicking you may be receiving right now, slow down.

Even just a little.

Breathe deep.

Pause during your day.

Soften.

Smile.

Place your worries into a virtual box and allocate a time you will address them.

Create time to take a break and allow yourself to linger there for a while.

Intention: Today, I will ....

Have you ever reflected on all you've been through and allowed yourself to acknowledge your strength?

Think of how far you have come, and all you have survived.

You've earned the right to look into the fire and smile.

Intention: Today, I will ....

Everything changes when you bloom through your next stage of growth.

The world sees you.

The sun shines more often, and you get caught in the rain a little less.

The wind whispers through the trees as you walk by, "There she is."

If you stop and be still for long enough, you will hear it too.

Then you can smile back and say, "Thank you."

Intention: Today, I will ....

Hanging on to resentment, anger and guilt is holding you back, influencing your decisions and potentially damaging your health.

You are the only one who can decide to forgive yourself and others, to set yourself free of the heaviness that holds your happiness to ransome.

If you have made some regretful decisions along the way in life, give yourself a little break and some love.

If you have been hurt by others, feel let down or ripped off, allow your lesson of the situation to be your focus.

It is not always easy to let something or someone go. It may take a little work.

There is transformation for you that waits in forgiveness.

It will be worth it.

Intention: Today, I will ....

To feel truly connected to your knowing, your heart, and your desires, get back to nature.

Disengage from walls, technology, noise, and routine.

Feel the peace flow through your cells as you allow the potency to heal and energise your body.

Inhale the breeze, allow the grass to ground your bare feet to the earth and feel the warmth of the sun on your skin. Stay there a while.

In the stillness, listen.

Your way forward is always revealed in what you hear in the peace and silence.

Intention: Today, I will ....

However you choose to behave and feel is what you will invite into your own experience.

The things that piss you off will be presented to you through other people so you can become aware of them, resolve them and grow.

If you feel annoyed and angry at someone else's actions, before you respond, consider what part of you they are reflecting.

What you do next, will determine the outcome of your interaction. It matters not what they do or say. It matters what you do.

Blaming others is the absence of self-love.

This next level willingness to take glorious responsibility for your happiness will transform your experiences in the world.

Intention: Today, I will ....

"What makes you happy doesn't need
to make sense to others."

Unknown

Even when you are winning at everything in life, smelling all the roses, savouring all the sunrises and singing to the stars, sometimes there will be a day in there that might not turn out so fab.

That's okay.

You can either choose to be consumed by it or be the observer.

Whatever is going on, there is always something good in each day to embrace.

The little things are the most powerful.

Choose to be aware of the good on those less sparkly days.

They will swing back around in no time.

Intention: Today, I will ....

Practice *is* perfect.

Loving yourself doesn't come from one grand gesture of one thing you did on one day.

Just like you wouldn't love your partner or child for only one day.

Loving yourself and living your best life comes from devoting time to actively practicing self-care and self-love every day.

Every, single, day.

Value yourself and give yourself permission to be your priority.

Intention: Today, I will ....

If you want to create change, you need to give yourself permission to do something different.

Interrupt the patterns you have shoved onto that *deal with later* pile. The time is now.

Decide what you are brave enough to confront and get uncomfortable with.

Who you are today only ever lasts as long as you allow.

Intention: Today, I will ....

Beautiful woman, you come first.

Before your partner, before your babies, before your family, and most definitely before your work.

Fulfilment and happiness can never be embraced if you make an agreement with yourself to be a martyr, to sacrifice your soul and to neglect your heart's desires.

To stand firm in your boundaries and self-worth means to connect with self-love.

Your relationships, successes and joys will weave into your greatest moments because you love yourself first and invite happiness into your world.

It is a beautiful dance with all that life has on offer and your radiant joy is a far greater gift to share of yourself than resented time.

Intention: Today, I will ....

You've likely heard many times, "Get your head in the game."

We are taught to think things through, make strategic decisions, be one step ahead of what others are thinking and leave the emotion out of it.

This style of creating and living, will no doubt result in great success for many. But then something else happens. You may either eventually end up in a job or business you don't enjoy, or you feel trapped.

Ultimately, these situations result in feeling disillusioned.

Recalibrate, through your heart.

The heart knows what the heart wants. Allow it to whisper to you.

This is alignment and authenticity, and true alignment creates magic.

Find stillness, listen, and find a heart led path to greater success and happiness.

Intention: Today, I will ....

In those moments when you feel that burning desire, say, "Yes!"

Yes to allowing yourself to come first.

Yes to the quiet moments of knowing exactly what you need.

Yes to the fear that stands on your chest and tries to hold you down, but you will do it anyway.

Yes to the not knowing how, but understanding that a deeply embodied guidance will lead you.

Yes to the freedom of letting go of judgement from others.

And yes to the risk.

Saying yes opens the realm of possibilities.

But make sure yes is for you, not others.

Oh, the sweetness of the joys that will follow.

Just you wait.

Intention: Today, I will ....

Happiness is determined by how you choose to view your world.

If you blame others, pass judgement, feel like a victim, complain, need to be perfect, berate yourself and spend your days feeling pissed off, you can most likely expect to feel less than chirpy.

However, if you take glorious responsibility, live through self-acceptance and self-love, embrace the growth in adversity, go with the flow, and smile at yourself in the mirror, if you aren't singing to the trees out of joy you soon will be!

Your happiness is always up to you.

Now, that is empowering. Feels better, doesn't it?

Intention: Today, I will ....

No doubt you've heard the saying, "Where your attention goes, your energy flows."

What you focus on, grows. It's Law of Attraction 101.

When we argue we give away our power and end up feeling angry, sad, and exhausted.

When you notice the negatives in life, you find more to notice.

You can take back control by choosing what you focus on.

Regardless of what you are experiencing right now, you can always, always anchor back to tiny moments of joy.

Where will your attention go today?

Intention: Today, I will ....

Answer those messages tomorrow. Maybe someone else can drop off little Johnny. Schedule time in your diary to sort the bills.

And allow yourself time to wash your hair!

Give yourself some time out and de stress.

You need it.

Intention: Today, I will ....

How much mental clutter are you hoarding?

Mental clutter means stress.

"What's for dinner, what time does little Johnny need to be at footy practice, how will I get my list done, who said what, have to answer all those text messages, need to water the garden, gas bill is due, fridge needs a clean out, what party on what date, urgh I need to get to the supermarket, the car needs a service, I don't have time to wash my hair, and, Omg I forgot Mary's birthday!"

We store crap in our minds because we don't create time to sort through it, much like that pile you've been avoiding.

Clutter creates stress.. stress creates clutter.

STOP!

For your own wellbeing.

Take time out. Deal with one thing at a time.

Say no.

"The purest form of happiness comes from loving every part of yourself. Even as a hot mess!"

Ali Williams

Sometimes it can feel like the days just keep coming around while we continue to pedal backwards.

It may feel like you aren't moving forward, but you are, more than you realise.

Acknowledge your growth. It may be subtle, but it flows through you.

Little habits and thoughts may have changed, or maybe you've created new experiences, attracted new friends and new opportunities.

Those new elements are your evolution.

Who you may be in another year is in creation right now.

Pretty cool, huh?

Intention: Today, I will ....

What new healthy habit have you been wanting to commit to?

Maybe you have already tried to start big, lost the motivation to keep going and have been beating yourself up for it.

The key is to start small, and repeat.

For example, consider deep breathing.

Set a reminder in your phone for several times during the day to take three, deep, slow breaths.

This action calms your nervous system, whatever you are in the middle of.

If you are at work, go to the bathroom and take the 30 seconds. If you are at the beach, take 30 seconds to inhale. Even in the middle of running the kids around, cooking dinner or drifting off to sleep, take another 30 seconds.

Do it every day, and build the habit until it becomes automatic.

You will start to value yourself more, and create new additional small habits that all go a long way to feeling great.

What can you start with today?

Intention: Today, I will . . . .

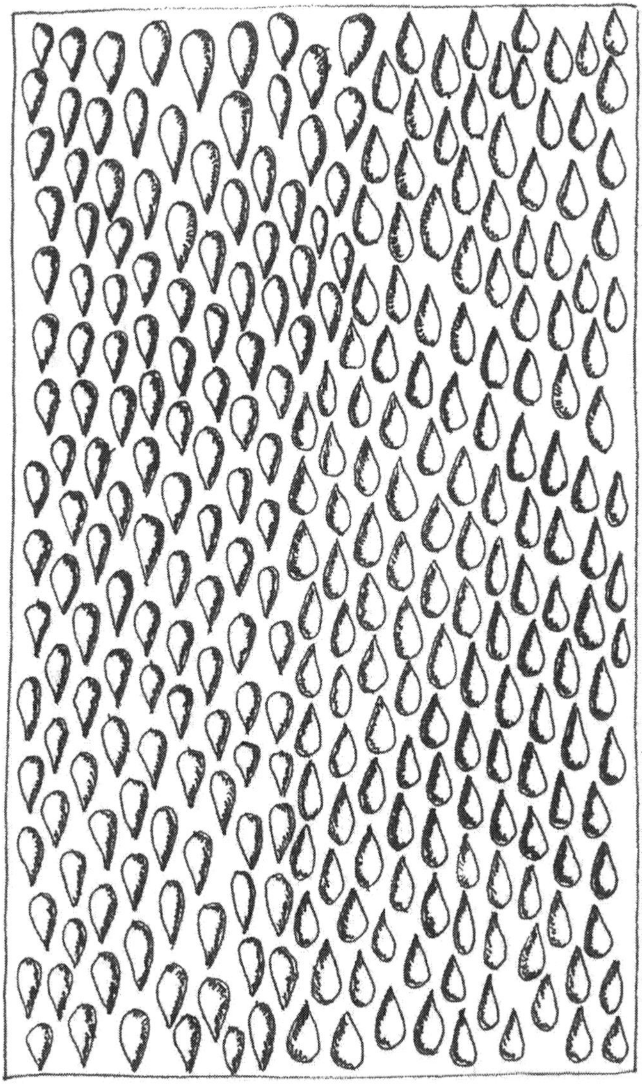

134

Your strength and joy are what gives life and love to this world.

In all that you do, all those you connect with, and each footprint you leave behind.

Intention: Today, I will ....

The most liberating moments in life occur when you release yourself from the obligation and expectation of others.

There is a difference between doing something for yourself or others because you feel inspired to, as opposed to feeling the dread of having to.

Say no more often.

Do the things that come only from your reservoir of love, and always for yourself first.

When asked to do something for someone else, first ask yourself, "Does this bring me joy?"

Your happiness is nurtured through alignment, not obligation.

Intention: Today, I will ....

Love is everywhere.

Open your eyes and look around with a deeper awareness.

Look for the signs in hearts that appear in nature, on tv, in magazines, on clothes, in coffee and other places you would never expect.

Once you see them, they can never be unseen.

Soon enough they will surround you everywhere you look, even where you've looked before.

It's a whole new world that will surprise and delight you.

Intention: Today, I will ....

Make the time to take the time for your health and wellbeing.

Get your bare feet on the ground and connect your body to the healing power of Earth.

Feel the fresh air and sunshine on your face and allow it to cleanse your senses.

Lay a little longer with a meditation to encourage healing of your cells.

Spend at least a few minutes on something creative and take a break from the practical grind to relax your brain.

Small powerful moments of connection to your own calm hold more magic than you can imagine.

Intention: Today, I will ....

You may never know the stories of the beautiful people who shine the brightest.

The traumas and hardships that have carved deep wounds in their souls have also created such 'Kintsugi' beauty.

'Kintsugi' is the Japanese art of repairing cracks in pottery with gold. It's about repairing the item in a way that reveals the gold to embrace the new beauty of the transformed cracks while restoring the function of the pottery.

When we experience adversity, we can either decide to be a victim or a survivor.

Everyone you meet has needed to make this decision at some point.

Look beyond another's presence to consider the journey that may be behind it. Maybe that person you admire has embraced their own *Kintsugi* to reveal their gold.

Intention: Today, I will ....

People who chase the dollar, or do what they think they *should* do, will often find themselves a few years down the track wondering what it all means.

Then the existential search for meaning begins through seeking out introductions with successful people, material possessions or a new jobs as a means to find fulfilment and relieve the feeling of emptiness.

Making choices that are not aligned with your values or passions will only ever lead to dissatisfaction.

On the other hand, if you go within, know your values, live authentically and understand how you can live in happiness, you will always feel a sense of purpose.

If you choose happiness first, your path will open up to opportunities that are just right for you.

And pathways that are right for you will bring you success.

Empowering yourself to make happiness your goal will bring magic and surprises that will astound you.

Go for it, what could you possibly lose? There are only amazing outcomes waiting for you to embrace.

Intention: Today, I will ....

Often, we will look for love and validation from other people to fulfil our worthiness.

We seek praise, acknowledgement and confirmation from our peers and family members to satisfy our longing for approval. It helps us feel like we *belong*.

What if you could be empowered by knowing that all the love and acceptance you need is already within you?

Take glorious responsibility for your happiness through loving yourself enough to acknowledge that you, your decisions and beliefs are enough, and you do not need approval from others.

Trust that you have all you need within you.

Intention: Today, I will ....

How someone behaves towards you, has nothing to do with you, and everything to do with them.

You are not responsible for anyone else's reactions, only your own.

You may be the switch. Your words or actions may intersect with another's *meaning* they have created through their own experiences in life.

Think of the scenario of hearing a song and it reminds you of a past event or person.

As humans, we make connections to particular actions and words, and because of our different upbringings, these patterns are created uniquely in each of us.

Don't take another person's behaviour personally. It is all theirs.

Intention: Today, I will ....

Those days when you didn't think you could take one more step, you did.

Those awkward moments in life that you've needed to dance around, has helped to build your resilience.

When you've thought you needed someone else to help you fix things, you did it on your own.

The times you didn't think you could breathe, you found oxygen.

And those days you felt heavy, were the days you grew your wings.

Intention: Today, I will ....

Choosing joy teaches your brain to look for more joy.

Choosing dissatisfaction teaches your brain to look for more reasons to be dissatisfied.

What would you like more of today?

Intention: Today, I will ....

"Smart women figure out what, exactly, makes
them the happiest. They spend generously
on those things but cut out the rest."

Laura Vanderkam

Are you as open to receiving love, as when giving it?

Giving of yourself to others is a wonderful quality, but if you give until you have nothing left, you are sacrificing the flow into your own being.

Sometimes we feel guilty accepting gifts, offers of support, or help from others. We can be very good at doing everything for everyone else but struggle to receive from others.

How often have you argued with a friend over who is paying for lunch?

Gracefully receive love from others with an open heart.

Welcome love, kindness, and generosity into your life.

Intention: Today, I will ....

There is something so beautiful about a woman who fully accepts who she is.

There is a certain special aura around she who gracefully dances through each day with a quiet mastery and calm reassurance.

Knowing and loving yourself allows a freedom from the restraint and obligation of expectation that too often gives the illusion of perfection.

Settle into who you are and breathe in your truth.

Intention: Today, I will ....

You don't always have to colour inside the lines!

Throughout our entire lives we are told how to behave, how to look, how to feel, and how we aren't good enough.

Somewhere in the midst of all of that we make agreements with ourselves that if we don't do things like everyone else, we don't measure up. And then we *shut* up because we fear judgement.

Give yourself permission to be you. Whatever you believe, and however you feel, it only needs to be accepted by you.

Don't be afraid to step outside the lines.

You just never know what potential you may discover.

Intention: Today, I will ....

To know and feel great happiness, is to have known and felt great sadness.

Without it, we can never understand what happiness is.

Don't hide your sorrow, but instead allow it to be a powerful force in treading your way through vulnerability to joy.

Intention: Today, I will ....

There was once a time in your life when nothing mattered.

All you thought about was chasing butterflies, running through the grass, and smiling at everyone.

Go back there in your thoughts.

Often.

That childlike innocence still exists, and with the wisdom of adulthood it's even more beautiful.

Intention: Today, I will ....

When it's all too much, you are too busy, your list is too long, and you just don't have the energy to face any of it, stop.

Give yourself permission to take a break, rest and let it go for a while.

The urgent can wait five minutes. Everything else can wait until you recharge and get your mojo back.

Take some time, guilt free.

Take responsibility for your boundaries and your wellbeing.

You'll be much more efficient when you pick it all up later.

Intention: Today, I will ....

We are all perfectly imperfect.

That's what makes us beautiful.

To accept all we are, allows us to be a powerful presence and show others the way forward.

Authentic women radiate a certain confidence that will not give in to self-criticism.

They have forgiven their imperfections and give themselves permission to be the most beautiful versions of themselves.

You have one body, mind and soul. Celebrate them and be amazed by your strength, wisdom, and bravery.

They are what make you, you.

Intention: Today, I will ....

There is only one of you.

How incredible is that?

It is amazing how each of us has our own unique identity.

We must cherish ourselves more and value our individualism.

There will never be another you. Even though we pass on our DNA and characteristics, we are not clones.

Appreciate how special it is to be you. And know your worth.

Allow your mortal presence to shine in this world.

Intention: Today, I will ....

Sometimes things don't go our way.

People don't always act the way we would like them to.

Disappointing events can catch us by surprise.

How do you react?

Do you take it personally, cast judgement and react emotionally?

Or do you choose to see the situation through love and know that you are not responsible for other people's behaviour, only for your own?

Peace, love and compassion first come from choosing to embrace them for yourself.

Intention: Today, I will ....

True kindness lives through your soul.

Kind people have an air of grace about them that radiates to everyone around them.

Every interaction they have with others seems to flow through compassion and understanding.

We need more kindness in our world. For our sake as humans, and for our children.

How can you embrace more kindness in your life?

It might seem like an effort to consciously show kindness towards others at first, but it can quickly become enjoyable.

Kindness achieves many things. Just look around.

Kindness can change people's worlds, including yours.

Intention: Today, I will ....

Stress is too familiar.

Short term stress motivates us to get the task done and can have a motivating effect.

However, prolonged stress is damaging to our health and wellbeing.

When we experience stress, our bodies go into fight or flight mode which affects many of our essential physical functions. Our digestive system shuts down, sleep hygiene is affected, our heart rate increases and hormones are overloaded, just to name a few.

All of those issues over the long term can put our health at serious risk.

The only ways the nervous system can regulate are to engage in activities that are calming, or restore during sleep.

Be aware of your stress levels, and remember that high levels on a daily basis are not the only option in your life.

Take action to prioritise your health and wellbeing and protect your body for the long term.

Intention: Today, I will ....

"I choose to make the rest of my life the best of my life."

Louise Hay

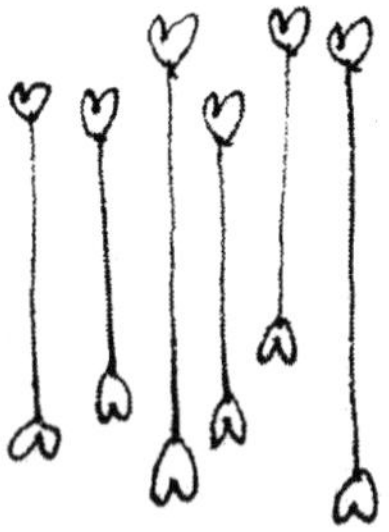

How you get out of bed determines the rest of your day.

Yes, some things are out of our control. But with your positive frame of mind, calmness, and willingness to go with the flow you will see problems resolve themselves, opportunities open up, and relationships deepen.

Before you put your feet on the floor, let go of yesterday, smile and acknowledge your courage. Say thank you out loud for all the good things in your life, decide what you want to achieve for the day, and breathe deep.

Feel the comfort and warmth of your bed, and notice the daylight peering through the window to welcome you into the new day.

Now you are ready.

Today is yours. Embrace it.

Intention: Today, I will ....

Do you ever allow yourself the time to consider all the amazing things in your world?

Perhaps instead of focusing on all you have to worry about, consider all the wonderful magic of our Earth.

Sit in nature and listen to the birds in the wind.

Breathe in the power of the ocean on a stormy day.

Appreciate the crops on the land that feed our communities.

Be thankful for all the mod cons available to us that make our lives easier.

Reflect on all the incredible serendipitous moments that have occurred in your life. You know those stories, they are the moments of unexplained magic.

Our world is filled with miracles, you are one too.

Embrace the wonder and see it in the small moments as well as the big creations.

They really are quite incredible.

Intention: Today, I will ....

Sometimes there is no amount of work you could do, or change you could create, that will make others happy.

It's not your responsibility either.

Maybe it's time to accept things the way they are and be the observer rather than the participant.

Yes, it is difficult when it is a close relationship. But you can choose to not engage in their negative reactions towards you.

You can still love them and wish them well, and you can also set boundaries.

They may not like it. Also, not your responsibility.

Embrace the energy of those who love you at your worst as much as they do when at your best.

As for everyone else, you don't need to give them all of yourself. You'll just end up dizzy when caught up in their own cycle of drama.

You only ever need to be gloriously responsible for yourself.

Intention: Today, I will ....

Too often we compare ourselves to others.

Someone else may seem to have it all. The success, the likes, the things, the job, or the relationship.

But focusing on what another has achieved and wishing you had the same only gives a false sense of your own authenticity.

Imposter Syndrome is a term thrown around a lot these days.

Feeling like a fraud or a failure is common.

How you live, love and work is all about you doing it *your* way.

It will never work trying to do it someone else's way.

Do things your own way, because your way is always good enough.

Intention: Today, I will ....

Remember you will always find your way.

Even when you're not sure what steps or direction to take next.

You are here, today, right now and this is your starting point.

Searching externally for answers about the big questions creates stress.

More the point, it emphasises the anxiety around the lack of clarity.

You can never force the decision that serves you best.

Take a step back and do nothing in the short term.

Be still, and silent.

Then listen to your inner knowing for the next step forward.

Intention: Today, I will ....

If you embody love, flow, trust and acceptance, your experience through adversity will be less painful.

If you are filled with bitterness and resentment... You get the picture.

Whatever you allow, will impact your reactions. It is also what you are inviting back into your life to experience more of.

If you were faced with a crisis today, how would you respond?

Intention: Today, I will ....

Eat the chocolate, drink the wine and dance naked in the garden!

Don't wait for someone to remind you, do it for yourself.

And if you have just read all that and thought, "Oh no, I couldn't," then you really need to.

Intention: Today, I will ....

Whatever is happening in life, it is important to embrace hope.

It's not about denial or avoidance, it's about acceptance and connection with your deepest self to make the best decisions for you, from here on in.

There is always something to look forward to.

It's only a matter of giving yourself the opportunity to open your eyes and think beyond the now, but also staying grounded and present.

Keep your ear to the ground for your next opportunity waiting to be called in.

It could be just around the corner.

Intention: Today, I will ....

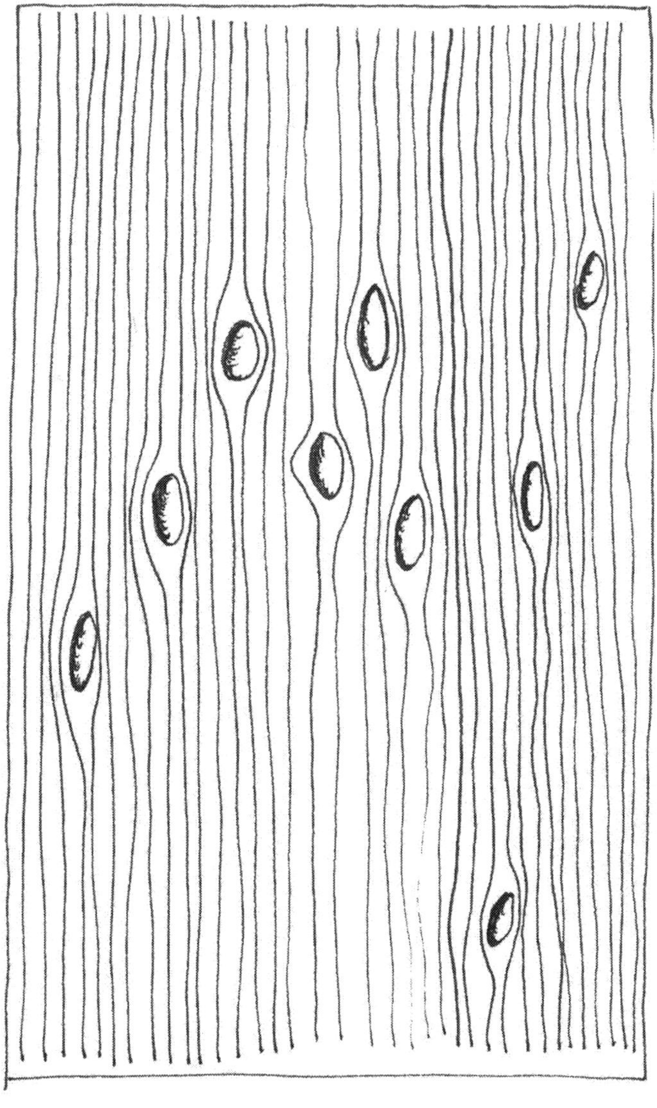

When something feels awful, know that there are always good things to come.

It is inevitable.

Ask yourself, "Is it a matter of life and death?"

If it is, take action to seek help and support.

If it isn't that serious but it still feels threatening, remind yourself you are safe, and take one step forward towards resolution today. And then another tomorrow.

Your nervous system may be firing out of control sending your body into fight or flight.

Take steps to regulate your body, mind, and soul.

And remember, the sun always follows the storm, just as much as the forest regrows after the fire.

Intention: Today, I will ....

There's a little known meaning in, "It takes one to know one."

To understand how this plays out in your life is to know yourself well and fully own it.

We have all repeated this saying so many times, but do you fully appreciate its meaning?

It means that what you see in others is a reflection of yourself.

If you see the beauty in your bestie, it's because they reflect your own beauty.

If you feel the love and connection for a partner, it is because you have love and connection to your higher self.

If you find yourself triggered by others actions, it is because they are showing you something to heal within yourself.

What you see in others, is what you see in yourself.

Knowing this, is to empower yourself.

Intention: Today, I will ....

No one can ever yell insults at you louder than your own inner critic.

The stories we have created and the agreements we have made for ourselves along the way have been holding us back and whispering lies.

It is time to give yourself permission to allow your true desires to silence the noise of the untruths that hide deep inside your being.

You can release those stories, embrace your whole truth and jump with both feet firmly planted in the realm of possibilities that await you.

Be willing to be the observer, get real and get comfortable with your new stories that move you forward.

Intention: Today, I will ....

"Happiness is not out there for us to find. The reason that it's not out there is that it's inside us."

Sonja Lyubomirsky

Allow time for your soul growth.

Growing into self-acceptance needs time to settle into your biology.

Replacing old patterns that have taken up space where love should live, requires forgiveness.

There is no peace in rushing.

Breathe deeply, love yourself softly.

Flowing through each day with a sense of grace while taking one step at a time will help you find your way.

Self-acceptance is your freedom.

Intention: Today, I will ....

Have the courage to go within.

Look around, don't be afraid.

There might be darkness, and it may feel frightening,

but you are the stars and magic happens there.

You may feel broken,

but you are strong.

Surrender to the beautiful adventure in the unfolding of the misunderstood.

Allow the illumination, the inspiration, and the elation.

Allow the glorious responsibility for your happiness to take you to where the mysterious meets the magical.

Intention: Today, I will ....

In any moment you can step into who you have always wanted to be.

You can focus on who you are right now and stay the same. Or you can focus on bringing the future to you and step into that.

Seems scary or don't know where to start?

Vulnerability, questioning, and doubting are always a natural part of the process before the leap of faith.

Trust that who you are meant to be is on the other side of your decision to move on from where it feels safe.

Step up and take ownership for what you want.

Give it some thought.

There are no guarantees of course, but isn't it better than things staying the same?

Intention: Today, I will ....

Some people are gonna be peeved when you start doing what's best for you.

Oh well, you can live with that. Really, you can.

No one else wakes up and walks in your shoes.

No one else is going to hand your future over on a fancy silver tray and wave a magic wand.

Only you can do what's best for you, guilt free, and confidently know exactly what you need.

Intention: Today, I will ....

Can you be alone?

Spending time by yourself is important. It allows you to just *be*.

It's not about kicking everyone out of the house so you can get the housework done.

It's also not about wanting to escape to the shops because you're desperate for some disconnection.

It's about moments of silence and calm, with no plans, no lists, no people, no phones, and no guilt.

If you already spend a lot of time alone, take the opportunity to find joy in the discovery of new hobbies and interests and just generally *be*ing.

Take time out. Steal it if you must.

Stop.

Breathe deep.

Protect and replenish your energy. Just *be* in your own company and enjoy the moment.

Intention: Today, I will ....

When you become consciously aware of your behaviours, you gain great insight into your thoughts and feelings.

Understanding and accepting yourself allows you to become an observer, rather than a critic.

Through this process you will empower yourself to learn and grow.

Ditch the judgement, show yourself some compassion and in doing so create opportunities for radical growth.

And radical growth only means one thing. A new pathway to happiness.

Intention: Today, I will ....

It's time to shift from surviving to thriving.

Self-care, self-acceptance and self-compassion all create self-love.

Self-love and self-actualisation lead to *thriving*.

When you are thriving, life gets exciting.

You attract more joy into your life, along with the people who will help you rise to a new level of excellence.

Take glorious responsibility for your shift from survivor to thriver and be wowed by the magic you will create.

Intention: Today, I will . . . .

Respect.

For you and your experiences.

Your pains and your pleasures.

Your tears and your laughter.

Your traumas and your celebrations.

Your stories and your secrets.

No judgement.

Only compassion.

You are nothing less than amazing.

Stop, for one second, and smile to yourself as you realise how far you've come.

Intention: Today, I will ....

Do you catch yourself complaining that you wish life was easier?

Staying in that mindset will continue to bring more of the same experiences in life.

Challenges *show* up to give you the opportunity to *step* up.

If you are never challenged, you will never change.

And life would be pretty ordinary if we stayed the same.

Embrace challenge, and allow the gold that brings the *glow* up.

Glow up is what all the cool kids say these days, beautiful. It's next level magnificence. Who doesn't want that?

Intention: Today, I will ....

Feeling beautiful today?

You should - you are!

Appreciate every lump and bump, every freckle, and every wrinkle.

Appreciate your strong body that carries you.

Love every part of you, no exceptions, and know that you are beautiful.

Intention: Today, I will ....

Do you care too much what other people think?

We all do, or have, at some point.

It comes from our inherent desire to be accepted because it feels good.

Humans like to be appreciated and recognised.

But, some will take the need more seriously and will seek validation from others and equate it to their self-worth.

Do you compromise your authenticity in this way?

You may stop yourself from doing or saying something if you feel you can't use your voice.

Don't let fear of judgement hold you back.

You will never please everyone, it's impossible.

It's irrelevant what others think of you.

Go forth and be yourself!

Intention: Today, I will ....

"No one can make you feel inferior
without your consent."

Eleanor Roosevelt

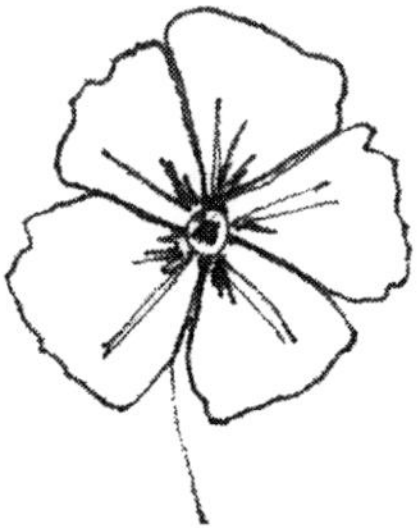

Balance: How do we find it?

We don't.

We must create it.

How?

The only way is through absolute, unwavering dedication to your own wellbeing.

It's about creating non-negotiable self-love and self-care practices.

Every. Single. Day.

It's about creating time that is all about you, only for you.

It's about recognising when you need to stop.

It's about recognising when you need to say, "No."

It's about choosing to live through joy.

It's about right here, right now.

It's about breathing deep, and being mindful.

Balance, starts with you.

Intention: Today, I will ....

There may be some people in your life who expect you to dim your light.

You may be too loud, too strong, too smart, too pretty or too successful for them to handle.

That's not about you, that's about their own insecurities that are too confronting to acknowledge.

Keep shining, beautiful. You are perfect the way you are.

Intention: Today, I will ....

Do you answer with, "I'm fine," when someone asks you if you are ok?

This response can become our default. Even when we long to share our deepest emotions with someone to not feel so alone, we don't, because it feels uncomfortable to be vulnerable.

But, every time you zip up another bag full of crap and add it to your already increasing load, you will eventually fall in a heap, and it could be some time before someone finds you buried under that mountain of baggage.

It's time to unpack your suitcase.

Release the burden of that heavy load.

Letting go of all that holds you down will open your heart and set you free.

Can you imagine, even for just one moment, what it would feel like to let it all go?

Intention: Today, I will ....

How *hard* are you trying to make things better?

Maybe it's time to ditch the hard and soften into allowing more joy, peace, and flow.

Did the penny just drop, beautiful?

Intention: Today, I will ....

Every day we are given the chance to choose who we want to be.

Who we decide to be, determines who we attract into our lives.

When you choose to be your beautiful, authentic self you will connect with people who will feel your vibe.

You know those moments. When you meet someone, and they don't feel quite right. Then there are the moments when you meet someone, and *shazam*! It's like you have known each other for years.

You attract aligned people when you allow your true self to shine.

Do more of that and your world will be filled with amazing people, just like you.

Intention: Today, I will . . . .

If you feel down, tell someone.

If you feel anxious, talk to someone.

If you feel fear, confide in someone.

If you feel hopeless, hug someone.

If you feel angry, offload to someone.

If you just don't feel quite right, acknowledge it.

Everything you feel is valid.

Honour it all.

Reach out to someone you trust, someone who has your back.

Know that you are loved.

Talking to someone is the first step. It might seem to be the hardest, but it is the bravest.

Intention: Today, I will ....

Your endless searching for fulfilment in that perfect partner, high achieving career, numbers on scales, or those new jeans, mean little if you lack the feeling of your own inner joy.

Take glorious responsibility for your happiness in creating it for yourself first.

You will find it in the simple moments, in the silence, in your knowing, and in your peace.

Everything else is the cherry on top.

Intention: Today, I will ....

Slow down your body.

Slow down your mind.

Slow down your heart rate.

Listen, to what your body needs.

Listen, to the silence.

Listen, to the calm.

Just be.

The insights and inspiration will flow.

Intention: Today, I will ....

There are people in your life who won't be who you want them to be.

You can't change them. You can choose to accept them, or not.

There will, however, be many people in your life who lift you up. Those people come when you recognise your own worth.

When you know your value, they see your value.

When you love yourself, they love you.

Intention: Today, I will ....

We don't always see the truck before it mows us down.

We may never have expected that sense of loss, shock, or misfortune.

But it has all stood for something. It has all been an opportunity for you to understand yourself at a deeper level to learn how to accept all that is, so you can grow.

What might not be going to plan for you right now? Remember that whatever is happening is presenting you with a choice. What you do with it will determine your experience.

Look within and see the learning.

Then you will know that all will be ok.

Intention: Today, I will ....

Never underestimate the power of the little things you do.

For they are not so little.

They set the tone for your entire life.

Value yourself and all you bring to the world.

You can only do that if you love yourself.

To love yourself, means you must always accept and forgive yourself for where you are.

To love yourself means you practice self-care in some way every day. No matter how small it may seem.

Remember the last time you threw a tiny stone into a pond, beautiful? Those big ripples go all the way, hey?

Intention: Today, I will . . . .

"Someone said to me many years ago, "You can have it all right now, if you want." I didn't comprehend what that meant at the time. Now I understand. It's all about knowing that having it all is choosing to. In this moment."

Ali Williams

You woke up today. Woo, winning!

You have the chance to decide what you want the day, week, and month to look like. For you.

You have the choice to make your own needs a priority.

Not every day is guaranteed to be rainbows and butterflies, but the sun will always set and rise.

So, take the opportunity to do something you have always promised yourself you would do.

If you want change, take the first step towards valuing yourself.

If you want peace, do something to turn down the noise around you.

And if you want to be able to smile, do something that brings you joy.

Intention: Today, I will ....

Whether you have chocolate or salad, enjoy it!

Give yourself permission to do whatever you need today.

Ditch the guilt.

Whatever you want is perfect.

Will the world end? No.

Don't beat yourself up.

What do you really feel like today?

Give yourself permission to do it and have it.

Intention: Today, I will ....

You have a choice, to be a victim, or a thriver.

You have the choice, to either seek out opportunity, or pass it by.

You have the opportunity, to choose positive or negative.

No choice is wrong, it's about asking yourself, "What serves me best right now?"

It's not about deflecting the challenging moments that are inevitable, but rather how you go through them.

Intention: Today, I will ....

More things don't make you a good person.

More things won't help you feel secure.

Attaching your self-worth to *things* leads to a repeating need for validation.

Wanting more is not the issue, wanting it because you feel a sense of lack reinforces dissatisfaction.

Stop and reflect for a moment. How much do you have in your life right now?

Celebrating the appreciation for all that surrounds you paves the way towards your happiness.

Maybe the "Jones's" feel like they never have enough. Fools they are to think *more* will make them happier.

Intention: Today, I will ....

When you walk, whether it be into someone's heart, or across the room, walk with intent and purpose that is for the benefit of all.

Intention: Today, I will ....

Sometimes we need soul feeding moments of silence.

To just be and breathe deep.

To stop, reset, centre yourself and get back in the flow.

It is a moment to appreciate all you are.

Silence brings peace, and it can bring the answers.

It will calm the mind and soothe the nervous system.

Take the time and sit in the quiet.

Your body, mind and soul will thank you.

Intention: Today, I will ....

Do you know your worth?

Do you stand strong in your personal power?

Being powerful doesn't mean being arrogant.

It means knowing yourself, accepting yourself and not compromising who you are for the sake of anyone else.

It means knowing your boundaries and standing in them firmly.

It is self-reliance, self-worth, and self-efficacy.

It doesn't mean you are a biatch.

To be powerful, means to be authentic.

Intention: Today, I will . . . .

We are all given opportunities to learn.

If we don't acknowledge the lesson the first time, we are given the chance to try again, but it will be harder.

Intention: Today, I will ....

Some days we feel invincible, and some days we feel afraid.

We can be strong, and we can be vulnerable.

Some days we will embrace the world, and some days we will hide from it.

While being amazing, we can also be fragile.

Allow yourself to be all of it.

Embracing your contrast is our superpower.

Intention: Today, I will ....

Nothing can begin until you ditch your fantasies of inadequacy, give yourself permission to decide what you want, and be who you are willing to step up and allow yourself to be.

Intention: Today, I will ....

We all wrestle with the parts of ourselves we don't like at times.

It is wrapped up in the need for perfection and the belief that we should be the complete package to be worthy and successful.

For all you wish you could change, someone else wishes they could be all you are.

What if you let yourself off the hook of expectation and disappointment?

Imagine how that freedom would feel.

Accept all that makes you unique, even the parts you doubt.

You're extraordinary. Every bit of you.

Intention: Today, I will ....

"The bottom line is that becoming happy is up to you. No one else can make you happy. And true happiness can never be built at the expense of others."

Tina Turner

Let go of the need to be in control.

Accept that all these moments have taught you a richness of growth.

Let go - and let be.

Intention: Today, I will ....

Allow yourself to let go.

Let go of past conversations replaying in your mind.

Let go of other people's choices to suffer. You cannot fix it for them.

Let go of the disappointment of those extra few kilos that have mysteriously added themselves to your waistline.

Let go of the need to be right.

Let go of your shame in saying something you wish you could take back.

Let go of the expectation of others.

Let go of all you haven't achieved and continue to beat yourself up for.

Let go of the partner who broke your heart.

Let go of the, "I wish I could," or the "I wish I had."

Let go of the anger attached to other people's behaviour.

Remember the time you wanted everything you have now?

Mic drop!

Intention: Today, I will ....

Babies smile at everyone because they don't yet understand difference.

Toddlers scream in public because they don't yet understand judgement.

Kids starting school clash with friends because they speak the truth before becoming a people pleaser.

Then something changes.

Along the way, while trying to figure out who we are, we filter our truths.

We do all the things we think we *should* do.

It can then take a while to find our way to our authentic self, if we ever get back there at all.

Your freedom in happiness is a certainty of choices to reconnect with who you really are and releasing the restraints of all the *shoulds* in life.

Intention: Today, I will ....

How did you wake up this morning?

Were you thinking about everything you must do, and everywhere you need to be?

Instead, wake up thinking about what you appreciate in your life.

It will give you a new perspective and a sense of peace.

Start each day with a new list of five things you are grateful for. Go beyond the obvious and go deeper.

There is power in the little things.

Do you like the smell of your first cup of coffee for the day? Add it to your list.

Part of taking glorious responsibility for your happiness is to alchemise the small moments of joy into a realm of magic in your present.

Intention: Today, I will ....

Guilt holds your past as your present.

Anxiety presents your future as an illusion.

Either way you are stuck.

Be present.

Your *now*, is your power.

Intention: Today, I will ....

If you woke up today thinking you can't, know that you can.

No matter what, you can.

Intention: Today, I will ....

You are not lost; you are only yet to realise you are already home.

You are not unsafe; you are only yet to realise your safety lies within you.

You are not lacking; you are only yet to realise you are all you ever need.

You are never alone; you are only yet to realise the world waits to embrace you.

And you are not flawed; you are only yet to realise you are exquisite.

You only need to accept that you are always, beautifully, quintessentially, perfect.

Intention: Today, I will ....

When you think about who you are, what is your language?

Your inner dialogue.

Do you speak kindly when describing yourself to others?

Do you whisper words of encouragement to yourself?

Acknowledge all that you are.

Fill in the blank, "I am................"

Intention: Today, I will ....

Let go of the need for perfection.

Perfect hair, perfect clothes, perfect makeup, perfect parent, perfect partner, perfect woman.

None of us can ever be all those things.

You are beautifully imperfect, and perfectly beautiful, just as you are.

Love yourself enough to accept that you are *always* enough.

Right here, right now, today.

Intention: Today, I will ....

What do you do consistently to take glorious responsibility for your own happiness?

Once off activities are great but won't create long term change.

Joy is created through empowering daily activities.

They don't have to be grand gestures. The simple things are always the best.

Love yourself enough to do something every day, just for you.

Intention: Today, I will ....

"Happiness is an inside job. Do not assign anyone else that much power over your life."

Mandy Hale

Every morning, your one waking question should be, "What wonderful and magical surprise will happen for me today?"

Revel in the anticipation, without expectation.

Embrace the magic, no matter how small.

Intention: Today, I will ....